THE NO
COMPLAIN
RULE

THE NO COMPLAINING RULE

Positive Ways to Deal with Negativity at Work

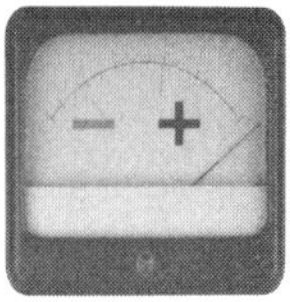

JON GORDON

International Bestselling Author of *The Energy Bus*

WILEY

John Wiley & Sons, Inc.

Published by John Wiley & Sons, Inc., Hoboken, New Jersey
Published simultaneously in Canada

For general information on our other products and services or for technical support, please contact our Customer Care Department within the United States at (800) 762-2974, outside the United States at (317) 572-3993 or fax (317) 572-4002.

Wiley also publishes its books in a variety of electronic formats. Some content that appears in print may not be available in electronic books. For more information about Wiley products, visit our web site at www.wiley.com.

Library of Congress Cataloging-in-Publication Data:

Gordon, Jon, 1971–
The no complaining rule : positive ways to deal with negativity at work/Jon Gordon.
p. cm.
Includes bibliographical references and index.
ISBN 978-0-470-27949-6 (cloth)
1. Employee morale. 2. Employees—Attitudes.
3. Negativism. I. Title.
HF5549.5.M6G665 2008
658.314—dc22

2007051635

Printed in the United States of America

F10012288_071919

For Jade and Cole

Always remember to choose the Positive Road

Contents

Acknowledgments

This book would never have been written if it hadn't been for Dwight Cooper, the CEO of PPR, who told me about the No Complaining Rule he implemented in his company and the positive impact it was having on his culture. This book is based on Dwight's commitment and dedication to creating a positive company where his employees create success and enjoy their work. Thank you, Dwight.

I also thank my wife, Kathryn, who inspired me to take the positive road in life.

Thank you to my maternal grandparents, Martin and Janice, whose last name I have passed on to my children. Thank you for your love.

Thank you to my parents for the greatest gift you could ever give me: your love. I miss you, Mom, but know that your spirit is with me.

Thank you to my agent, Daniel Decker, who supported this project from the start and helped make it a success.

Thank you to my editor, Matt Holt, and to Kim Dayman, Jessica Campilango, and the wonderful team at John Wiley & Sons for making this book possible.

Thank you to the other members of my team who work hard and never complain: Jim Van Allan, Cathy Garwood, Brooke Trabert, and Amy Walter.

Thank you to all my clients who allow me to work with your companies, organizations, teams, and individuals. I am grateful every day to get to work with so many wonderful people.

I also have to give a big thank you to the managing partners at Northwestern Mutual who supported our No Complaining Tour to benefit Pediatric Cancer. Thank you to Tim Bohannon, Tait Cruse, Matt Russo, John Wright, Bob Waltos, Joey Davenport, Harry Hoopis, Scott Theodore, and John Goodwin.

I'd like to thank Ken Blanchard for his continued support of my work. Ken, you have played a major role in my life both professionally and spiritually. You have the purest heart I have ever known and I'm honored to know you.

Most of all I'd like to thank the original creator of the No Complaining Rule, God. Thank You for the inspiration to write this book. You deserve the credit.

Introduction

A Simple Rule Is Having a Big Impact

I didn't invent the rule. I discovered it—at a small, fast-growing, highly successful company that implements simple practices with extraordinary results.

One day I was having lunch with my friend and client Dwight Cooper, a tall, thin, mild-mannered former basketball player and coach who had spent the last 10 years building and growing a company he cofounded into one of the leading nurse staffing companies in the world. Dwight's company, PPR, was named one of *Inc.* magazine's Fastest Growing Companies several times, but on this day PPR was named one of the best places to work in Florida and he was sharing a few reasons why.

Dwight told me about a book he had read that dealt with jerks and energy vampires (negative people) in the workplace. But after reading and reflecting on the book, he realized that when it comes to building a positive, high-performing work environment, there was a much more subtle and far more dangerous problem than jerks. It was complaining and more subtle forms of negativity, and he knew he needed a solution.

Dwight compared jerks to a kind of topical skin cancer. They don't hide. They stand right in front of you and say, "Here I am." As a result you can easily and quickly remove them. Far more dangerous is the kind of cancer that is subtle and inside your body. It grows hidden beneath the surface, sometimes slow, sometimes fast, but either way, if not caught, it eventually spreads to the point where it can and will destroy the body. Complaining and negativity are this kind of cancer to an organization, and Dwight had seen it ruin far too many. He was determined not to become another statistic and *The No Complaining Rule* was born.

I Was a Professional Complainer

Now before I share a story of how the No Complaining Rule works, it's important that I let you know that just because I wrote this book doesn't mean I'm some Mr. Positive, Pollyanna, smile all the time, happy guy who is never negative and never complains. In fact I used to be a professional complainer. I blamed everyone else for all my problems. I didn't like me and I didn't like my life. I complained about my house, my lack of success, my wife, my weight, my lack of money, and just about everything else. In fact if you've read my book *The Energy Bus*—a fable about a guy who is miserable, negative, and whose wife is about to leave him—you should know that the character was based on me. My complaining and negativity got so bad that my wife gave me an ultimatum. Change or I was off the bus. I was dejected, rejected, and about to be ejected!

The fact is, complaining was a big part of my life and upbringing. I often joke that I come from a long line of complainers. I grew up in a Jewish-Italian family with a lot of food and a lot of guilt—a lot of wine and lots of whining. My grandmother was full of love for her family but full of fear in her life. She was so scared of flying, she would say, "I know when they say your time is up, your time is up, but I don't want to be on a plane when someone else's time is up." And every time I would see my aunt she would start off the conversation with what was wrong with her life. To this day I still get e-mails from her saying "Hi" and then listing her problems. Even birthday cards to my children say, "Happy Birthday, Wish I was not dealing with so many problems so I could enjoy it with you." But I don't blame my family. As I said, I come from a long line of complainers. After all, my ancestors walked around the desert complaining for 40 years. In a trip that should have taken 11 days, it took them 40 years. Talk about inefficiency. But that's what complaining does.

There's even a passage in the bible where the Israelites are freed from Egypt by Moses. They had spent 400 years as captive slaves and now they were free. At first they were happy and thrilled. But within a month and a half they started complaining about being hungry. They complained about not having enough water. They complained about living in the wilderness. They even said it would be better to be back in Egypt as slaves rather than be free in the desert. Three hundred years of slavery, and all it took was a month and a half to start complaining again. Finally, God got so frustrated with all the complaining that He threatened their very existence. Turns out God is a big proponent of the No Complaining Rule. I would even venture to say that God originated it.☺

It turned out that my wife wasn't a big fan of complaining either. Even though complaining was ingrained in my DNA and the cards were stacked against me, when she threatened the very existence of our marriage I had no choice but to take a long, hard look at my life and realize how my complaining and negativity were manifesting in everything that was wrong in my life. I was dying every day instead of living. I came to agree with Abraham Lincoln that "A man is about as happy as he chooses to be." And so I began to research the positive effects of being positive and the harmful effects of being negative. This led me to write, speak, and consult with businesses and organizations and this ultimately led me to the No Complaining Rule.

Do I still complain? You bet I do. Just a whole lot less. Do I still get down? Of course. We all get down, but the key is how we turn it around. Every one of us will face negativity, energy vampires, and obstacles on the road to success. That is why one of the most important things we can do in business and life is to stay positive with strategies that turn negative energy into positive solutions. Thus the goal of this book is not to eliminate all complaining, just mindless, chronic complaining. And the bigger goal is to turn justified complaints into positive solutions. After all, every complaint represents an opportunity to turn something negative into a positive. We can use customer complaints to improve our service. Employee complaints can serve as a catalyst for innovation and new processes. And our own complaints can serve as signals that let us know what we don't want, so we can focus on what we do want. In this spirit I share with you a story about the No Complaining Rule and other positive ways to deal with negativity at work and at home.

THE NO COMPLAINING RULE

Chapter 1

Hope

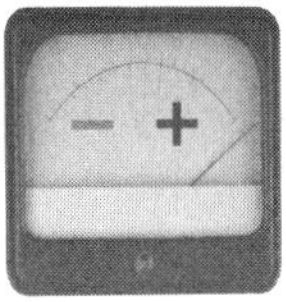

It was Tuesday, and Hope dragged herself into the office just like she had every day for the past year. She walked past security with her head down, stumbled into the elevator, and slapped her face a few times after the door closed. For some reason her morning pot of coffee wasn't doing the usual trick. She was late, and thankfully this meant that everyone was already at work and the elevator was empty. She was suffering from another sleepless night, a swollen head, puffy eyes, and worst of all . . . a broken heart.

She thought of the various routes she could take from the elevator to her office. If worse comes to worse, I'll make a mad dash for it, she thought. She wasn't ready to talk to anyone yet, and she certainly didn't want anyone to see her until she could carry on a normal conversation without crying. Besides, she was Vice President of Human Resources for EZ Tech so it wouldn't be long before they came in droves to her office anyway—to talk, to gripe, to dump their problems and issues on her. She was part manager, part psychologist, part peacemaker, and part garbage can. It came with the job, and she accepted all of it.

She really did like helping people; however, lately she had trouble listening to their problems. As they would talk, all Hope could think about were her own problems. She read their lips, but all she thought was, If they only knew what I was dealing with. If they only knew about my life. If they only knew. . . .

Chapter 2

On Fire

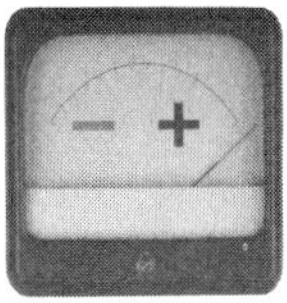

The elevator opened, and the loud noises startled Hope. People were running everywhere in all directions. Phones were ringing off the hook. The marketing and PR teams were running into each other in the halls. Everyone was screaming across the room. We are either under attack or the market has crashed, she thought. Not today. I don't need this today, she cried to herself as she quickly walked with her head down toward her office. Before she could take another step, she looked up and Jim was running at her.

"Hope, Hope, Hope. Where have you been?" he shouted as he approached her face to face.

"I heard my name the first time," she said, hoping he would back up a few feet, or a few miles for that matter. He had the worst coffee breath in the world, and her stomach was already feeling queasy.

"Yeah, well, maybe I'm just happy you're here," he countered. "Or maybe I'm just in complete shock that on one of the worst days in our company's history you are nowhere to be found. Our boss is on national television having to explain why our computer batteries are catching on fire, and you're strolling into the office an hour late looking like you've been hit by a bus."

I feel like I've been hit by a bus, Hope thought.

Jim grabbed Hope's arm as he rushed her into his office and pointed at a chair as he directed her to sit down.

"In all my years in charge of operations I've never seen the media descend on a company like they have with this story. They are like a bunch of attack dogs. The Business Television Network (BTN) just finished their interview with Dan, and the street is not acting kindly. Millions of people just watched our CEO take a verbal beating on air. Our stock is plunging, and we've got to figure this out."

"We've had problems before with our hardware. We've had glitches. I don't see what the big deal is this time," Hope said, shaking her head.

"It's more than that," said Jim. "The battery issue is just the tip of the iceberg. Everyone's saying that Dan has lost his way with the company. And would you believe the interviewer had the nerve to ask Dan what it was like to go from a rock star CEO to being called a has-been whose company stock is at an all-time low? BTN brought up the fact that we have bloggers within our company who are bad-mouthing management and even posting memos that we have shared with our employees. Can you believe it? Private memos being shared with the world? Now we look more like zookeepers than computer makers. Personally, I'd like to do a seek-and-destroy mission today and find out who those people are and escort them out of the building myself," Jim said, gritting his teeth.

"We will. We will," answered Hope, trying to calm Jim down, knowing his temper often got the best of him.

Chapter 3

Morale

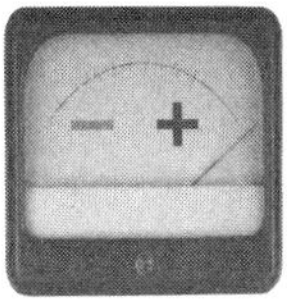

The irony was too perfect, Hope thought. Here she was feeling like she just wanted to scream at the top of her lungs about the unfairness of her life, and she was the one having to calm Jim down. All she wanted to do was get to her office, close her door, put her head in her hands, and fall apart, but as usual she had to help someone else keep it together.

She knew that when Jim was fired up, the best thing to do was to calm him down by agreeing with him and then share alternative ideas later. Thankfully, her caffeine boost was kicking in, and her adrenaline was flowing. She was starting to think more clearly. Jim was a hard charger, take-no-prisoner kind of manager who liked order and results. They certainly would have to find out who these bloggers were, but there was more to the story. She was the bridge between the executive team and thousands of employees, and she didn't need anyone on national television to tell her that they had a morale problem on their hands. She had approached Jim and Dan several times about their issues and even offered suggestions to improve the culture, but as usual it was put aside as a "good idea" for the next meeting because there were more pressing issues to be discussed. Logistics, sales, call center problems, customer complaints, stock price, shareholder meetings—everything was always more urgent than their employees' concerns, so negativity kept spreading and morale kept getting worse. After a while she grew tired of saying anything. Besides, she had enough problems of her own to deal with that she certainly wasn't going to fight to solve her company's problems if no one wanted to listen.

Sure, everyone would get excited after attending a leadership seminar and talk about being positive and building a positive company and they even sent out positive messages to the employees via e-mail for awhile, but by the time the next crisis hit, everything would go out the window. It was all about the stock price. She wished she had a dollar for every time Jim, Dan, or a member of the executive team had mentioned the words *shareholder value, stock price*, and *market expectations*. She had ideas and solutions, but Jim was the biggest obstacle to getting any of them implemented. Jim's idea of building a positive culture was buying the employees pizza once a month.

She tried to talk to Dan about making their culture a priority, and he would listen but nothing would get done. Why should they change anything? The stock price was at an all-time high. They enjoyed record profits the previous year, and everything was looking good. Real good. That is until today. Today, their dirty laundry was being shown to the world, and it didn't look good at all. Maybe now they'll finally realize that even though we make computers, we are not run by computers. It's a people business, she thought. Hopefully, today they would see that.

9

Morale

Chapter 4

The Phone Call

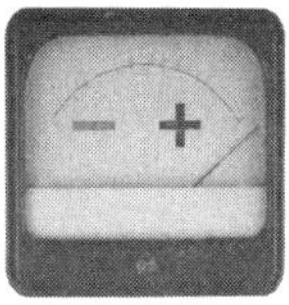

Wayne and Ken hurried into Jim's office almost knocking each other over. They were as different as two people could be. Wayne was the VP of Marketing for EZ Tech. He was a fast-talking northeasterner with wavy dark brown hair that was slicked back to expose his good-looking face. He was as straightforward as they come and made it clearly known that he desired to be a CEO one day. He was quick to share his ideas and suggestions and even quicker to shoot down the stupid ideas of others. Ken, on the other hand, was a mild-mannered southerner who headed up Manufacturing for EZ Tech. He spoke slowly and methodically and listened more than he talked.

As different as they were, however, today they were both sweating and nervous. Hope knew that neither of them had ever been through something like this before. Their involvement would be critical in handling this crisis, and Hope was curious to see how they would respond. She observed people and learned a lot about them just by watching. As she expected, Wayne spoke first, "I just got off the phone with Dan, and he'll be calling in about two minutes. I see everyone is here but Robert." Just like Wayne, Hope thought. Always trying to get control of the room and situation by identifying who's there and who's not. A regular master of the obvious. Everyone knew Robert was overseas closing a big sale with a government client.

"Shall we all sit down?" Jim asked as he motioned for everyone to take a seat.

The phone rang, Jim pressed the conference button, and Dan greeted everyone with a calm welcome. He was a tall, thin, mild-mannered CEO whose focused, calm demeanor was shaped by his years coaching college basketball. He eventually left his job as a basketball coach to start EZ Tech with a college buddy, but as Dan told Hope many times before: "I didn't leave coaching; I just chose a different arena to apply my principles." And, ironically, his leadership, coaching skills, and ability to handle pressure were being put to the test like never before.

Dan continued, "So as everyone knows, it's been a very challenging and interesting morning. I certainly haven't enjoyed being ridiculed on national television in front of the business community and my peers. I don't like that the credibility of this company and our great team is being questioned. We have certainly been knocked off our pedestal, and I am determined to do whatever it takes to solve our problems and regain the admiration and trust of our customers and the market. The world is watching, all eyes are on us, and how we respond will say everything about who we are and what we stand for. And so I ask you right now: Who is ready to take on this challenge with me?"

Everyone in the room responded in the affirmative.

"So let's tackle the issues one by one. First and foremost we need to address our battery problem. Jim and Ken, what are your thoughts on this?"

"Obviously we need to find the flaw," answered Jim.

"Great. And what else?"

"A recall?" Ken added, unconvincingly.

"No doubt about it," responded Dan. "Let's get on it immediately. Fix the problem and replace every battery with a new one. It will cost us now, but it will save our reputation and our future."

As usual Wayne jumped into the conversation. "I was thinking that we should also put together a three-point plan to share with the media explaining how we will address the battery problems and the other issues brought up on BTN today."

"I'm not surprised you had already thought of this, Wayne," laughed Dan. "And you are 100 percent right. We'll announce the recall immediately and then let the media know we are creating a three-point plan to address our challenges, and we will have it to them by Monday. And then we'll create a more in-depth plan to share with our board of directors who are very concerned—as they should be. This brings us to the issue of the bloggers and all the negative things about our company that are being leaked to the media. We have to do something about that. Any ideas?"

"I plan on having Hope find out who those bloggers are ASAP," Jim said with a raised, angry voice. Everyone stared at Hope, and she could feel them judging her. Her eyes were clearly still puffy and since it wasn't allergy season, it was clear to all that she had been crying again.

"We need to find the bloggers and talk to them," countered Dan. "But there's a bigger problem here than just a few negative bloggers. You see, in all my years of coaching, whenever I had a problem on my team I didn't blame the players, I blamed myself. And right now the media is right. I feel like we have lost our way, and I haven't done a good job coaching. I've ignored the very principles I have used to create successful basketball teams and to build this company. Today hit me like a sledgehammer, but it woke me up. I know what our problems are, and today we begin the process of finding and implementing solutions."

Chapter 5

The Real Problem

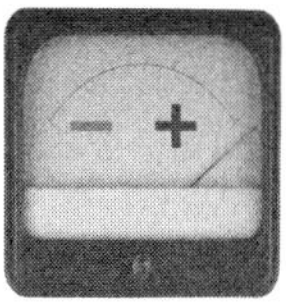

"You see, team," Dan said passionately, "our problem is negativity, and we have no one to blame but ourselves. I believe where there is a void, negativity will fill it. And, unfortunately, within every organization you get voids in communication between leaders and their employees and between different teams and team members. It happens everywhere: with sports teams, work teams, family teams. Within these voids, negativity starts to breed and grow and, eventually, like a cancer it will spread if you don't address it. As an executive team it's up to us to do everything we can to prevent these voids from occurring and when they do occur, we must quickly fill them with positive communication and positive energy. People don't just want to be seen and heard. They want to hear and see, and if they don't feel like they are part of the company then they will assume the worst and act accordingly.

"Hope has come to me many times with suggestions to improve our communication process and improve our culture and to address our people's concerns and, quite frankly, I have not listened well or acted. As a result, we have created far too many voids that have allowed negativity and morale problems to fester, ultimately manifesting into our current crisis. This is not a problem of a few negative bloggers. They're just a symptom. So is our battery problem. Our real problem is negativity and our negative culture, and we need to address this immediately."

"Got it," said Jim. "I'll get on this immediately."

"No, Jim," responded Dan. "I want Hope on this. You got that, Hope."

"Yes sir," she said as Jim glared at her and her heart sank. She volunteered enthusiastically, but deep down she felt like she couldn't even manage her own life, never mind helping Dan fix the company.

"That's great, Hope. I want you to put together a plan to address our negativity problem and our culture by Monday. I'll highlight it as part of the three-point plan we present to the media and also share a comprehensive, detailed plan with the board. So get started immediately, Hope, and I'll be in your office tomorrow to discuss this further."

Hope smiled as everyone in the room shook their heads in disbelief.

Chapter 6

Traffic

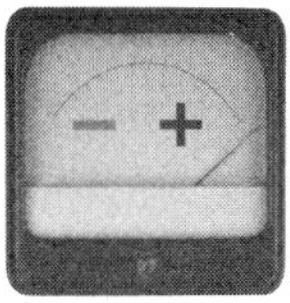

Hope lived only 25 miles from work, but the usual traffic made it feel more like 60 miles. In the past she used the extra time on the way home to listen to leadership and inspirational CDs, but lately all she did was review the list of complaints she received from employees that day and generate a list of her own—and traffic was at the top of her list. If people would just look at the road and drive like normal people instead of looking at the wrecked cars on the side of the road, we wouldn't have traffic, she thought. Why do people have to be so clueless? You should have to take a "clueless" test before receiving a driver's license, she convinced herself.

"What are you doing?" she yelled out her window as the driver next to her tried to cut in front of her. "Just stay in your own lane. Don't you see I'm here!" I pity the person who tries to mess with me right now, she said, looking at herself in the rearview mirror. I can't believe Dan wants me to come up with a plan to save the company from negativity, she thought to herself. I can't even save myself.

She didn't know how much more she could take. Just yesterday her doctor told her that he detected something "of concern" in her yearly physical and wanted to run some more tests. She knew that breast cancer ran in her family and was terrified that she would be the next one in her family to get it. As she drove home inch by inch, stopping and going, she thought about her doctor's appointment the next day and tried to figure out how she would fit it into her schedule, knowing how adamant Dan was that she create a plan by Monday. After the year she'd had, she certainly didn't want to tell anyone about one more problem in her life. She needed the job to support her two teenagers and also knew she was lucky to work with a leader like Dan. He was the one man in her life who wasn't a jerk. She debated whether she should tell her children about her medical tests and decided to wait until she received the results. They had been through a lot this past year, and it was clearly taking a toll on all of them. Just last night when she walked in the door, she and her daughter got into it once again.

"Where were you, Mom?" Lauren yelled.

"That's a nice way to greet your mother," countered Hope. "Where do you think I was? At work like I am every day, trying to support us."

"Did you forget about the homecoming dance this Friday?"

"No, I didn't, Lauren, but let's just say I have a lot on my plate right now."

"Well, I don't have a dress, and you promised we would get one together."

"Just go naked," said Jack as he giggled and made faces at his older sister.

"Be quiet, you little punk," she said as she took a swipe at him. "You're 15 years old now. Stop acting like you're 10."

"This week is a little crazy, Lauren. I may just have to give you money to go pick one out yourself. I'm sorry."

"Yeah, me too, Mom. Everyone else's mom is helping them. I don't even want to go to Homecoming this year. I don't like my school. I don't like my friends, and I don't like not having a dress."

"Don't be such a complainer," countered Hope. "You sound like the people I work with."

"Complainer! Complainer! You're calling me a complainer!" countered the strong-willed 17-year-old. "That's all you do is complain. You walk in the door and complain about your job. You complain about all the people complaining to you. Then you get on the phone with Grandma and Aunt Pam and complain to them for most of the night. All you do is talk about how bad life is since Dad left. He didn't just leave you, Mom. He left us, too. And we're still here. So every time you say how much you hate your life, it's saying that you hate your life with us. If I'm a complainer, it's because I had a good teacher."

Hope couldn't even respond. Lauren definitely was her mother's daughter. Payback, she thought, for all the hell she put her own mother through. She grabbed a bottle of wine and locked herself in her room. She thought about her ex-husband, who told her he wanted a new life and a new wife. She thought about the mountainous credit card debt he left her with. She thought about the bills that were piled on her desk. She cried herself to sleep last night only to come into work today and face a firestorm of negativity and batteries on fire.

And as she drove home, reflecting about last night, she wondered what else could go wrong. "What else do you have for me?" she asked, as she looked up and clenched her fist. As the traffic eased up a bit, Hope thought of the enormity of it all. She was fired from her marriage and now trying to keep her job. Her relationship with her daughter was falling apart. And who knows what the medical tests would reveal tomorrow.

Not to mention Dan's expectations of her. She didn't want to arrive home tonight and fight with her daughter again, and she didn't want to go to work tomorrow, either. She wanted to escape and run away. If my ex can do it, why can't I? she asked herself. She wanted to tell Dan that she had too many projects to contribute to his three-point plan and would recommend that Jim run with it. She convinced herself she would tell this to Dan first thing tomorrow.

Hope finally made it home, walked in her front door, and was surprised to find a quiet, empty house and a note. It was from Lauren letting her know that she was at her boyfriend's house and Jack was at a friend's house eating dinner, and they would be home later. Thank God, she thought. She didn't have the energy. She poured herself a glass of wine, did some research on the computer, then found her way to the couch where she eventually passed out.

Chapter 7

The Talk

Hope was proud of herself. She was only going to be 10 minutes late today. She knew Jim would tell Dan about the condition she was in yesterday, and she knew Dan was going to come see her in her office so she wanted to be as early and prepared as possible. But when she arrived, Dan was already sitting in her office waiting for her.

"Hope, Hope, Hope."

Why does everyone have to say my name three times? she thought.

"What a surprise," he said. "I didn't think I'd see you for another 45 minutes."

"Very funny, Dan."

"I'm not being funny," he said, staring at her. "I'm dead serious. You know this is a very critical time for me and our company. I have to get this bus moving in the right direction, and I need to know if you are on it."

"Of course I'm on it. I just don't know if I can figure out the answers to our problems right now. I'm not in the best state of mind and my life. . . ."

"Listen, Hope. I know you have had a tough year ever since your husband left. I know it's not easy raising two teenagers all by yourself. You know I've been there for you, but I've realized there comes a point when my kindness is detrimental to all of us. If I don't challenge you you're not going to grow, and if you don't grow you can't help us grow."

"But what about Jim? Wouldn't he be better suited for this right now? He's itching to make something happen. I just don't know if I'm the best person for this and. . . ."

"Jim has his strengths, and you have yours. People are most energized when they are using their strengths toward a bigger purpose and there's no bigger purpose than saving our company. This job is not for Jim. I know your strengths, and this job is for you."

"I just need some more time to get my life together," she said with her head down.

"No, Hope. You don't need more time. Enough of that thinking. The time is now. I believe everything happens for a reason. This battery crisis will make us a stronger company, and I believe your taking on this challenge is exactly what you need right now. You see, Hope, ever since your husband left you've been like a wounded animal who's only concerned about yourself and your life and your problems. You went from someone who wanted to help everyone in the company and change the world to someone who just wanted to hide and wallow in self-pity. That's not who you are. I've watched you for awhile now and tried to give you space to sort it all out, but I can't do that anymore. It's not good for you or me. It's time to let your bags off the bus. Let go of the past. Stop being disappointed about where you are and start being optimistic about where you are going. Focus on the future. Move beyond yourself. Instead of focusing on your own problems, focus on helping others with theirs. This is what you do best. This is who you are. Use your strengths for a bigger purpose and help me save this company."

"You're a hard person to say 'No' to," Hope said, knowing everything he said was true.

Dan smiled. "Remember, Hope, *what we need the most we resist the most.* And right now you need this and we need you. What do you say?"

Chapter 8

The Cost of Negativity

"Okay, I'll give it my best shot," she said, knowing she really didn't have a choice. When Dan was convinced of something, it happened one way or another. He would do it with her or without her, and if it was without her then that meant she would be without a job. She couldn't afford it. Not now. And besides, she didn't want to disappoint Dan. Several years ago he recruited her with relentless enthusiasm and gave her the opportunity of a lifetime. Then in the midst of all her personal struggles he stood by her through thick and thin. Working with Dan was the best experience of her professional life and she wasn't ready for it to end. She owed it to him. Yet she was also full of fear. She had done some research the night before and discovered the magnitude of the problem they were facing.

"But you need to know it's not going to be easy," she said, holding up a piece of paper.

"Nothing worthwhile ever is," Dan responded.

"I did some research last night, and here's some real data on the cost of negativity. This is not just our problem. I'd call it the biggest problem in business, and it not only affects us as an organization but it affects us individually." She handed him a piece of paper that read as follows:

Cost of Negativity

- Negativity costs the U.S. economy between $250 to $300 billion every year in lost productivity, according to the Gallup Organization. And this number is conservative since it doesn't take into account the ripple effect of complaining and negativity.
- Ninety percent of doctor visits are stress related, according to the Centers for Disease Control and Prevention, and the #1 cause of office stress is coworkers and their complaining, according to Truejobs.com.
- A study found that negative employees can scare off every customer they speak with—for good (*How Full Is Your Bucket?* by Tom Rath).
- Too many negative interactions compared to positive interactions at work can decrease the

productivity of a team, according to Barbara Fredrickson's research at the University of Michigan.

- Negativity affects the morale, performance, and productivity of our teams.
- One negative person can create a miserable office environment for everyone else.
- Negative emotions are associated with the following:
    - Decreased life span and longevity
    - Increased risk of heart attack
    - Increased risk of stroke
    - Greater stress
    - Less energy
    - More pain
    - Fewer friends
    - Less success

Dan looked over the sheet of paper and nodded. "This is a great start. You see, I knew you were the person for this job."

Hope smiled.

"Now that we know what we're up against, we can create a plan to win the battle." He continued, "If there is one thing I've learned in all my years of coaching it's that you need to know your competition, and once you know them you can exploit their weakness. Negativity has a weakness. Let's find a way to exploit and conquer it, and we'll be well on our way to a successful turnaround."

The meeting was over, and as Dan walked out the door he turned around and said, "And, by the way, Hope, I want you to know that I believe in you. I know you can do this."

A tear fell down Hope's cheek because she was so thankful there were still good men left in the world. Now if only I could believe in myself, she thought. Hope tried to gather her thoughts about what to do next. I have no idea, she thought. No idea at all.

Chapter 9

It Could Be Worse

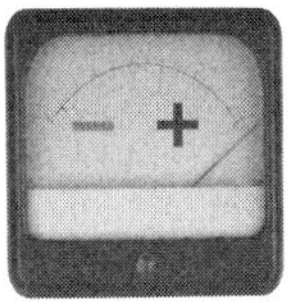

Hope walked outside the office building, hoping some fresh air would clear her head. Dan certainly had motivated her, but she knew all the motivation in the world wouldn't help her if she couldn't create a plan that the executive team could execute. She sat on a park bench in front of her building and watched people get on and off the bus. She noticed the #11 bus and wondered why people were always so happy when they got off. Don't they know they are heading into work? I wish someone would just throw me in front of a bus right now. That would make everything easier, she thought. Hope was in such deep negative thought that she didn't even notice the security guard who had been standing in front of her for a few seconds. He tapped her on the shoulder.

"Miss? Miss? Hope?"

Startled, Hope responded, "Excuse me, can I help you? How do you know my name?"

"I know everyone who works in this building, Miss. And I know you know who I am. Because up until about a year ago you used to walk past me every day and give me a big smile before you got into the elevator. I have to tell you that it was the highlight of my day. Your smile was like a ray of sunlight coming through on a dark, dreary day. Now all you do is walk past me and ignore me like everyone else. Like I'm not even here. I might as well be a statue. I have to be honest with you, Miss, your smile was the best part of my day and I miss it. I figure I'd come out here and try to cheer you up so I can see your smile again. I know you probably have some problems in your life like everyone, but I'd like to tell you a story if that's okay with you."

"Sure," said Hope, who wasn't sure what to say.

"You know Snoopy? As in Charlie Brown and Snoopy? Well, it was Thanksgiving and Charlie Brown was enjoying a feast with his family. Poor Snoopy wasn't invited. Snoopy was all alone on his doghouse with dog food and a dog bone. He wasn't a happy camper. But then he had a thought that changed everything. He thought, 'It could be worse. I could have been born a turkey.' You see, Miss, I don't know what you're going through, but I hope you'll remember it could always be worse.

Thanks for listening. I hope to see more of your smiles again."

The security guard gave her a big smile and headed back into the building. Hope rubbed her face and ran her fingers through her hair.

She thought of what Dan said earlier about how she had been so consumed with herself. She didn't even know that a simple smile had such an impact on someone else. What else did she not know? How many other people had she affected at work by being consumed with her own miserable life? Maybe Dan was right. Maybe this was her chance to get back to making a difference again. Maybe by focusing on saving her company, she would save herself . . . and benefit others in the process. She knew she needed to get started immediately, before heading out early to the hospital for the tests.

Chapter 10

Cancer

Hope drove to the hospital as quickly as possible. She was scared, and when she was scared she drove and talked fast. She tried to take her mind off the tests she would be having by thinking about how they should deal with the negative bloggers at work. She thought about the research she shared with Dan on negativity. It occurred to her that cancer exists in both bodies and organizations. Yes, she agreed with Jim that these particular bloggers were jerks and she knew that, unfortunately, jerks existed in every organization. She thought of them as a kind of topical skin cancer. They don't hide. They stand right in front of you and say, "Here I am." As a result you can easily and quickly remove them. Far more dangerous is the kind of cancer that is subtle and inside your body. It grows hidden beneath the surface, sometimes slow, sometimes fast, but either way, if not caught, it eventually spreads to the point where it can and will destroy the body. This is the kind of negativity she was concerned about at EZ Tech and knew it would destroy the company if she didn't figure out a way to solve it. With morale and their stock price at an all-time low, they needed an answer and quickly.

The No Complaining Rule

Hope's hand shook as she wrote her name on the sign-in pad at the hospital registration desk. She took a seat and waited for what seemed like an eternity to be seen. She hated hospitals, and even worse she hated waiting in hospitals. She didn't have anything against the people who worked there. She just considered herself allergic to needles, blood, pain, and people in white coats. To Hope, nothing good ever came from being in a hospital. She looked around and couldn't believe she was there. I don't need this, she thought. Why me? Why now?

Finally, a large, imposing woman stood in the doorway and called her name. Hope walked toward her and mumbled, "It's about time" to herself.

"Sorry for the wait," the woman said. "We are just so backed up today. But I'll make sure you get in and out of here as quickly as possible."

"Great," said Hope. "I have to get back to work and I've already been here longer than I wanted to be."

"Like I said, I'll do my best," the woman responded as she brought Hope to a private room and looked at her chart. "You are Hope, right?"

"Yes," Hope said, annoyed. Who else would I be, she thought.

"We just have to make sure I got the right chart. Sometimes they mix the charts up, and you never know. I just love your name. My name is Joyce, but I always wanted a name like Hope. My older sister is named Joy, and I always wished they had named me Faith, Hope, or Grace or something like that. But my Daddy loved the name Joy so much that when I was born they called me Joyce. Isn't that funny? Joy and Joyce."

Hope interrupted, "So how soon can we get these tests going? I don't even want to be here and. . . ."

Joyce smiled. She knew she had another wild one on her hands. "No one wants to be here," she said. "But you *are* here, so let's do what we have to do. First I'm going to take some blood and get it over to the lab, and then we'll send you off for an ultrasound; it's that simple."

"Great," Hope said, her hand still shaking. "Did I tell you I hate needles?"

"No, you didn't, but I'm not surprised. Tell me what else you don't like."

"Are you serious?" asked Hope.

"Sure," said Joyce. "I just love hearing people complain. It's the best part of my job," she said with a big sarcastic laugh.

But Hope took Joyce's invitation as an opportunity to unload everything she hated about her life. "I don't like that I'm here. I don't like that I may be sick. I don't like that my husband left me. I don't like that my teenage daughter is 17 going on 30. I don't like that my credit card bills are bigger than my savings account. I hate traffic. I hate hospitals. Should I continue?"

"No, that's good," said Joyce. "And now that we played the game 'Ain't It Awful?,' I want you to look at that sign over there."

Hope looked over and it said, "NO COMPLAINING."

Hope shook her head, feeling embarrassed.

"Well, Hope, you said your piece and now I'm going to say mine. I have a No Complaining Rule around here and starting now I'm invoking it."

"But I'm in a hospital. I have every right to complain," Hope said, raising her voice.

Who does this woman think she is? Hope thought, as she grew steadily angrier. She has no idea what I'm going through. She doesn't know what it's like to know that the test you are about to take will determine your fate. But Joyce did know. She had worked with thousands of patients and did her best to care for all of them. She didn't create the No Complaining Rule for herself, but for them. She knew that there were two main reasons why people complained: (1) because they were fearful and helpless and (2) because it had become a habit. With Hope it was both reasons. Joyce knew people felt helpless and out of control when they came to the hospital, and she saw the No Complaining Rule as a way to get their attention and empower them with a different perspective. She wanted to help them take the positive road. She only hoped that Hope would be willing to join her on it.

Chapter 11

The Positive Road

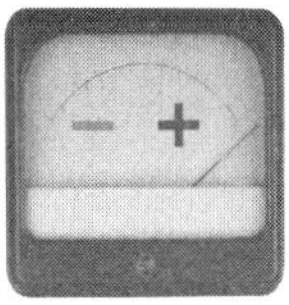

"You have a right to complain," Joyce said. "I can't stop you. It's a free country, but it's like my sister Joy who drives a bus says, in life you have a choice between two roads. The positive road and the negative road. The positive road will lead to enhanced health, happiness, and success and the negative road will lead to misery, anger, and failure. Since your bus can't be on two roads at the same time, you must decide which road you want to be on. And when you complain, you travel down the negative road. So which road are you on, Hope?"

"I think it's pretty clear," Hope said as she calmed down a bit. "But when you feel the way I do, it's as if the positive road is closed with a big sign that says Do Not Enter, if you know what I mean. And besides, what about venting?" Hope asked. "Sometimes you need to let it out. Sometimes a person just needs to complain. You hear psychologists say it all the time. That it's healthy to vent, and if people don't have an outlet, then it's bad for their health. Ironic don't you think, since you work in a hospital?"

"The psychologists are wrong!" shouted Joyce, raising her hand in the air.

"They are right about one thing. We were born to complain. As babies, we cried our hearts out to get what we want. When we were hungry, we cried and our Momma fed us. When we were tired, we cried and we were rocked to sleep. We cried to get our way all the time, and it worked like a charm. Unfortunately, far too many are still using an adult form of crying—called complaining—to get what they want or to express their feeling of helplessness. But just as we learned not to suck our thumb and sleep without a night-light, we must also outgrow the habit of complaining. There are certainly better and more productive ways to deal with our negative feelings. Sure, we all need to complain once in a while. Everyone does. But, Hope, I've got you pegged, and you are not a one-time complainer. You sound as if you've had a lot of practice. And there are millions of people like you. I call them CCs—Chronic Complainers—and they're not only hurting themselves but annoying everyone else. It's like the great football coach Lou Holtz said, *'Don't complain. Eighty percent of the people you complain to don't care and 20 percent are glad you have problems.'*"

Hope went from angry to sad very quickly. She knew Joyce was right, and she knew her daughter was right. She was a CC. The writing was on the wall. No wonder so many people avoided her lately. They didn't want to listen to her.

Joyce continued, "No matter what the psychologists say, complaining doesn't make us feel better. Maybe temporarily, but in the long run complaining creates a cycle of negativity that feeds itself and grows. Think about it. For years psychologists had their patients hit punching bags to relieve anger only to find out recently that this practice creates more violence. It works the same with complaining. When we complain, we feed the negativity. You know what I'm talking about, Hope? Some people wouldn't have anything to say if they weren't complaining."

"Yeah, like me," Hope answered with a look of despair. "You know, it wasn't always like this. I used to be an eternal optimist. I used to be the one all my friends called to cheer them up. Then he left me. Then he crushed my heart. It's just like you said. As time went on I became more negative. I grew more bitter and angry every day, and now look at me. The fact is, I feel like I'm dying every day instead of living. I used to believe in miracles and signs that guided me in the right direction. Now the only miracle I wish for is for the strength to get out of bed in the morning."

"It's okay, girl. You can quit any time you want. As my sister says, you can get off the Complain Train and hop on the Energy Bus any time you want. You can get off the negative road and hop on the positive road right now. The positive road is never closed. And if you ever get off of it, you can always get back on.

"What do you say? Let's go get you that ultrasound and while we're at it, we'll hop on the positive road together."

"Sure," said Hope, who was surprised at her response. She was about to learn her fate and was facing the possibility of really bad news. Yet Joyce made her feel better than she had in a long time. She just hoped her test wouldn't give her something else to complain about.

Chapter 12

The Complaining Fast

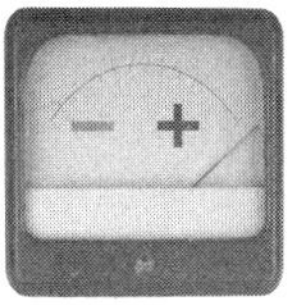

Silence filled the air as they sat waiting for the ultrasound technician.

"It's really easy to quit, you know," suggested Joyce.

"Quit what?"

"Complaining, silly. Everyone can do it."

"Even me?"

"Oh, I've seen much worse than you quit in a flash. Cold turkey. It's a simple two-step process. You want me to tell you what it is?"

"Sure," said Hope, knowing she didn't have anything to lose and besides she didn't want to think about the ultrasound for one more second.

"First in Step 1, you do a No Complaining Day. I call it a complaining fast. You quit cold turkey. It's great because it causes you to monitor your thoughts and realize how negative you really are. When I did this, whoa, I was shocked at the stuff that came out of my mouth and thoughts that popped into my head."

"Sounds like I need more than a day of no complaining," Hope said. "How about a no complaining year? Does it work for kids and employees too? That would be a godsend."

"It works for everyone," Joyce said. "You'll get to a year eventually. But start with a day. Then go for a week. Then a month, then a year. Like any bad habit, it's a one day at a time kinda thing, and remember change begins with you. I know because even as I tell you this, I still complain myself but just a whole lot less. Which brings me to Step 2. When you do complain, because you most certainly will—everyone does—use your complaining to your advantage. You see, every complaint has an opposite. If there is something you don't like, then there is something you do like. If there is something you are not happy about, then there is something that would make you happy. Complaining can actually be a gift if we use it correctly. If we pay attention to our thoughts, words, and complaints, we will learn a lot about what we don't want and don't like. We can then use what we don't want and don't like as a catalyst to help us determine what we *do* want and *do* like. The fact is, we will never completely eliminate complaining from our life. The key is to turn complaining against itself and make it work for us. Instead of letting it generate negative energy, we can use it for a positive purpose. We can use complaints as a 'signal' or 'sign,' letting us know we are on the negative road and then in the next moment we can take a detour to get on the positive road. Each time we catch ourselves complaining, we can say, 'Okay, I don't like this or I'm not happy about this. So then, what do I want? What will make me happy? What thought will bring me peace instead of frustration? What actions can I take to rectify this?' Let your complaints tell you what you don't want, so you can focus on what you do want. Every complaint represents an opportunity to turn something negative into a positive. We can use complaining as a catalyst for positive change in our own lives, at work, and in the world. So I say, 'Let your complaints about problems move you to solutions.'"

"I'm with you," Hope said. "I understand what you're saying. And it sure sounds simple when it's just you and me talking in here, but I have a feeling that breaking the habit isn't so easy when you are dealing with the stuff of everyday life. Especially at work, when you're stressed to the max."

"It's easier than you think," said Joyce, "but you have to have tools. Not like a hammer or anything, although some complainers could use a hammer to the head to change their thinking, but I'm talking about techniques that help us create positive habits. It's all about the tools."

Joyce gave Hope a little card that described the three No Complaining Tools and said, "Here you go, sweetie. Just use this card, implement the tools, and you'll be well on your way on the positive road. As for me, I've got to go see my other patients. But first I'll find out where your ultrasound technician is. I'll tell her to get her butt here and quick," she said with a big laugh. "Oh, and before I leave I want to give you this," she said as she reached into her pocket and pulled out a rubber bracelet. I got it from my church and it says STAY POSITIVE on one side and THE NO COMPLAINING RULE on the other. You wear it, and it makes a great reminder not to be a CC. Let's face it. In this world we need all the positive reminders we can get."

As Joyce left the room, Hope put on the bracelet. She wanted to complain that the ultrasound technician hadn't shown up yet but instead found herself reading the card with the three No Complaining Tools. This was a good thing, since she would need all the positive reinforcement she could get.

Chapter 13

Three No Complaining Tools

The card looked like this:

1. **The But → ___ Positive Technique.** This simple strategy helps you turn your complaints into positive thoughts, solutions, and actions. It works like this. When you realize you are complaining, you simply add the word *but* and then add a positive thought or positive action. Example:
    - I don't like driving to work for an hour *but* I'm thankful I can drive and that I have a job.
    - I don't like that I'm out of shape *but* I love feeling great so I'm going to focus on exercising and eating right.
2. **Focus on "Get To" instead of "Have To."** Too often we complain and focus on what we *have* to do. We say things like "I have to go to work." "I have to drive here." "I have to do this or that." Instead, shift your perspective and realize it's not about having to do anything. You get to do things. You get to live this life. You get to go to work while so many are unemployed. You get to drive in traffic while so many don't even have a car or are too sick to travel. Focus on what you get to do. Focus on feeling blessed instead of stressed. Focus on gratitude.
3. **Turn Complaints into Solutions.** The goal is not to eliminate all complaining. The intent is to eliminate the kind of mindless complaining that doesn't serve a greater purpose and allow complaining that is justified and worthwhile. The opposite of mindless complaining is justified complaining. The former is negative and the latter is positive. The difference is intent. With *mindless complaining,* you are mindlessly focusing on problems; however, with *justified complaining* you identify a problem and the complaint moves you toward a solution. Every complaint represents an opportunity to turn a negative into a positive.

Chapter 14

No News Is Good News

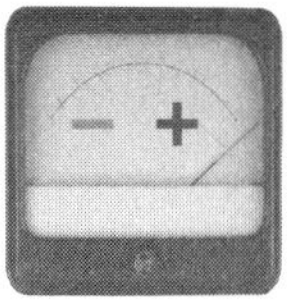

As Hope drove into work the next day, she found herself wanting to scream. But as she looked at the bracelet on her wrist, she remembered Joyce's No Complaining Tools and tried to shift her perspective. She couldn't forget that yesterday she had to wait another 30 minutes for the ultrasound technician to arrive after Joyce left, and, to make matters worse, no one would tell her if the ultrasound showed anything. She was told that the doctor would be in the next day, and someone would give her a call either Friday or Monday with the results of the ultrasound and blood work. Blood work takes longer, they said, and the doctor would want to have both reports before calling her. They act so casual about it, she thought. Here I wait for hours in the hospital, miss work, and they don't even give me an answer. Sure, it's not a big deal to them. It's not their life hanging in the balance. They see a hundred people a day just like me, and I'm just a number to them.

Hope found herself going down the negative road fast. She thought of the No Complaining Tools and inserted the word *but,* trying to think of something positive. But I met Joyce. She didn't treat me like a number. She was great. And as they say, no news is good news. Hope thought of the No Complaining Rule. Yesterday when she left the hospital, she went straight home. When she arrived, her daughter started one of her usual rants, but Hope stopped her and invoked the No Complaining Rule. They talked about it as a family, and Hope, Lauren, and Jack all decided to try a One-Day Complaining Fast and see how it went. Hope wasn't sure how it would go for all of them today, but she did know one thing. It worked last night with her daughter. Now if it could work with EZ Tech employees, we're in business, she thought. She had a lot of great ideas brewing but wasn't quite sure how they all fit together. She would create a plan today. Today it would all come together. At least that's what she hoped.

Chapter 15

Fundamentals of Prosperity

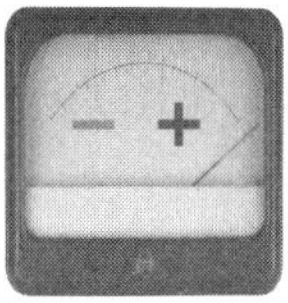

Dan was sitting in Hope's office again when she arrived. Fortunately for Hope, she was five minutes early to the shock of everyone in the office. She could tell that Dan was in business mode and wasn't there to chitchat. She had worked with him long enough to know his "I want answers" face.

"Listen, Hope, you know I don't like to micromanage anyone, especially you, but Jim is real concerned that you won't be able to deliver the plan we need. I just need to check on your status. He said he looked for you all afternoon yesterday and you weren't here."

"I was at the doctor's," Hope responded. "Maybe next time I'll bring Jim with me so he can hold my hand."

"That's fine, Hope. I just need to know you're on it."

"I am. I have a lot of great ideas coming together and. . . ."

Dan interrupted, "That's great, but we don't just need ideas. We need a plan. I need to share a brief statement with the media about our plans on Monday morning, and I present to the board of directors Monday at 2. I need to know that you will deliver. Everyone's wondering if you will get the job done, and I'm telling them that I have faith in you, and with all we have going on right now I need to be able to count on you."

"You can count on me," Hope said, assuring both Dan and herself. "I'm working on it all day today, tomorrow, and over the weekend. You will have it first thing Monday morning."

"Good. Good. Good. But I expect you to get a lot done today because tomorrow I want you to update the executive team on your ideas and have a rough draft of your plan. We'll also be checking on the status of the recall and repair of our batteries. I told the team you'll be ready, so be ready."

"I'll be ready," said Hope, who *hoped* she was telling the truth.

"Excellent," said Dan, and he handed her a book titled *Fundamentals of Prosperity* by Roger Babson. "And while you're working on your plan, I want you to consider this. I was looking for inspiration last night and found it on my bookshelf. I read it a few years ago and started reading through it again, and one part really spoke to me and our situation. Interesting, since it was written in the 1920s. It's where the author was interviewing the president of Argentina and asked him why South America, for all its natural wonders and resources, still lagged far behind North America in terms of prosperity and progress. The president thought for a moment and said, "I have come to this conclusion. South America was discovered by the Spaniards in search of gold but North America was settled by the Pilgrims in search of God.' It made me think about what we are searching for and what our motive is as a company. We focus so much on stock price, profits, and gold that we ignore the spirit and culture of our company. As you know, great companies and teams have great energy and spirit that are fueled by a positive culture and purpose, and it seems we have moved away from this. I hope your plan will address this and help us get back on track."

Dan's words were music to Hope's ears. She had been telling him this all along. But as she knew all too well, it doesn't matter how many times someone tells you something, often you need to find the answer for yourself in your own time. And right now it was clearly Dan's time.

"My plan will address this loud and clear," said Hope. "It's like the root and fruit of the tree. So often we focus on the fruit (results, profits, stock price, etc.), and that's all well and good since we need to measure them and be held accountable.

But if we focus on the fruit too much at the expense of ignoring the root (our people, culture, teamwork, and spirit), then eventually the root dries up and so does the fruit. That's what happened to us. We ignored the root, and it rotted on national television in front of millions of people."

"You have that right," said Dan, who cringed as he remembered the worst day of his professional life. But that cringe quickly turned to a smile as he picked up an apple that was sitting on Hope's desk. He could feel the energy shift. Things were turning around, and he grew more confident in Hope and in his decision to put her in charge of this initiative. Jim was certainly seeding his mind with doubts, but in his gut Dan felt Hope would deliver. He just wished the executive team felt the same way, and he looked forward to Hope proving them wrong. As a basketball coach he loved walking the sidelines, picking one of his subpar players, and sending him into the game to the surprise of his teammates. The look on the player's face as he ran onto the court was one of complete shock. Like a deer seeing headlights. But sure enough that player would often do something wonderful to the shock of everyone and help the team win. After doing this a few times, every single player would be mentally and physically prepared because they never knew if their coach would send them into the game. And it also taught a valuable lesson. Never doubt your teammates, because when they're under pressure they will do something amazing. Now it was Hope's turn. She was the least likely person to be picked from the sidelines and now was her chance to shock everyone.

Chapter 16

The Bloggers

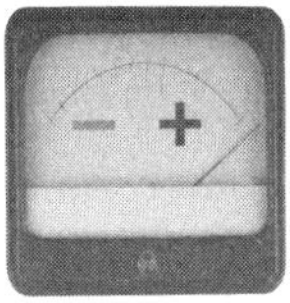

Hope and Dan finished their discussion by talking about the bloggers and creating a plan of action. They now knew who they were, and Hope went to meet with them and deal with the situation. One of the bloggers was clearly remorseful in his conversation with Hope and told her that he was only revealing his frustration with management's disregard for him and his team's effort. He was angry and just wanted to express how he felt because he didn't think he would be heard any other way. But he surely wasn't expecting his blog to receive national attention and had no intention of hurting EZ Tech. He wanted to remain with EZ Tech, so he agreed to shut down his blog after Hope explained to him that the company was addressing his concerns.

Hope's meeting with the other blogger didn't fare as well. He made it very clear that EZ Tech deserved all the negative publicity it was getting and that he and just about everyone he knew at the company didn't trust management. Even after she explained that they were creating a plan to address his issues, he was too bitter to work with her to create solutions. He said he would continue his blog and if the company didn't like it, too bad. Hope knew that he was right that many employees had lost their trust in management. It was the company's leadership's fault but she also knew that he needed to be let go. He was too focused on the past and unwilling to move forward.

Hope never liked having to let anyone go, but she knew that in the process of building a positive culture you had to let some energy vampires off the bus, as the saying goes. Every year EZ tech would have to do this. She remembered reading a report where a hospital let go of a few negative doctors each year and in the process enhanced morale and profits. Turns out the negative doctors were scaring away a large number of patients. After her experience at the hospital yesterday, she wasn't surprised. She also knew that each year Robert, the head of sales, had to let go some of his negative sales and customer service people. Robert always said that one person can't make a team, but one person can break a team. And worse, negative people can scare away every customer you have. It is hard enough to succeed in today's world and no one wants negative influences holding them back.

Pink slips would always be necessary, she thought, but there has to be a better way to deal with negativity. After all, no matter how many negative employees we let go, there will always be new ones to take their place. We'll always have to deal with negative employees, so I've got to come up with a better way to attack negativity before it attacks us, she said to herself. She knew the answer would be key to her plan, but what she didn't know was that it would come from an unlikely and surprising source.

Chapter 17

The Yard Guy

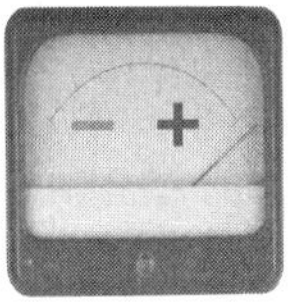

After a very productive day, Hope arrived home from work feeling like her plan was coming together. There were a few missing pieces, but she would try to address them tonight after dinner with the kids. Before heading into the house, she stopped to talk to the yard guy, who was applying his magic organic mixture to her lawn. Hope could barely afford to pay a yard guy, but she was sick and tired of always yelling at Jack to fertilize and mow the lawn, and besides, the fines from the neighborhood for an unkempt yard were more expensive than paying someone to take care of it. They had weeds everywhere, and something had to be done. At Lauren's request, she decided to go with a yard service that didn't use chemicals or pesticides. Hope got a kick out of her daughter. Most parents were worried about their kids getting into trouble, and all her daughter talked about was green initiatives and global warming and measuring their carbon footprint. Lauren was adamant about not using toxic chemicals.

She tapped the yard guy on the back, who was crouched over looking at the grass. He pulled a few pieces to show Hope. "It's working just like I said."

"Yeah, about that," Hope said. "I was wondering how in the world you can eliminate the weeds and prevent them from taking over my lawn without chemicals when everyone in my neighborhood uses chemicals to treat their lawn."

"Well, you see, I have a different approach. What I do is treat the lawn with an organic mixture that creates an environment where the good grass can grow healthy and strong. Then it grows and spreads to the point where it crowds out the weeds, and the weeds have nowhere to grow. *It's all about the environment.* Takes a little longer and a little more work up front, but once you have the good grass growing good and strong, it spreads like kudzu and then you have an amazing, vibrant lawn. Makes everything a whole lot easier, and it's less expensive, too. Instead of spending all that money on chemicals, you simply continue to support a healthy environment."

Hope couldn't contain her enthusiasm. She hugged the yard guy and called him a genius. No one had ever called him a genius before. "Weird," maybe, for putting garlic on someone's lawn, but genius, never. But he very much liked the sound of it. And to Hope he was a genius because he provided the missing and key piece to the first part of her presentation.

Chapter 18

Friday

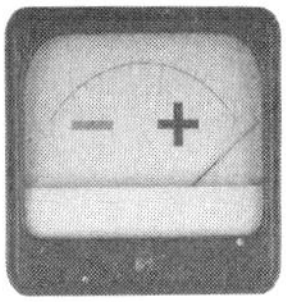

It was Friday, and Hope should have been tired. But she wasn't. She felt more alive than she had all year. She was fueled by the fact that her presentation magically came together at 1 A.M., and she was excited to share it with the executive team. She was also thrilled that she, Lauren, and Jack had another wonderful night together. She thought of them as she sat in her office and smiled at the fact that Lauren had made a No Complaining poster and put it on her bedroom door. *I should do that here at work,* Hope thought, and she smiled even more.

Day 2 of their No Complaining Fast went very well, and at dinner they agreed to try it for a week. "A whole week, YES," shouted Jack as he pumped his fist in the air. When Hope asked her children what they liked about the No Complaining Fast, Lauren said she was happy to see her Mom smiling again and talking about positive things, and Jack said he was just glad he didn't have to hear his Mom and sister fight anymore. Yet Hope knew they liked the No Complaining Rule for a far bigger reason. Things were starting to feel normal again, and they could sense it. They just wanted their life back the way it was. Even though I can't make things exactly the way they were, at least I can give them the very best of myself, Hope thought. She walked over to her bookshelf and pulled out a book that inspired her several years ago. She loved just taking a book off the shelf, opening it randomly, and reading the page she opened to. She felt whatever she was supposed to read would be right there for her and this time was no exception. The book said,

Stay Positive

It's easy to be positive when everything in life is going great. The hard part is staying positive when you get knocked down and kicked around. The fact is, no one goes through life untested. If you study history, sports, and business, you will find that every great leader and team had to overcome adversity and challenges to define themselves and their success. With so many people telling us we can't do it, we have to be positive and believe we can. We have to have faith and trust in a bigger plan

> for us and our team. The concept of the "overnight success" is a myth. Life is a test, and a deciding factor of whether we pass or fail is the answer to the following question: "Are you going to stay positive in the face of your doubts, fears, and challenges?" Staying positive is not about putting on a fake smile or believing you can do it all yourself. Rather it's about being optimistic and living with hope and having faith. The measure of our success will not be determined by how we act during the great times in our life but rather by how we think and respond to the challenges of our most difficult moments.

Reading this made her think about the challenges that lay ahead. She didn't want the results of her tests to throw her kids off track again. She vowed that no matter what happened at work or at the hospital she would stay positive for her kids and herself. I fell apart once. I can't fall apart again. She then thought of Joyce, which she had been doing a lot the last two days, and in that same moment coincidentally the phone rang and it was Joyce on the other end of the line.

"I was just thinking about you," said Hope.

"I'm not surprised," said Joyce. "Listen, about the results. . . ."

Hope's heart began to race.

"I'm sorry we don't have them yet, but I just wanted to let you know I was thinking about you and praying for you. We'll have results for you definitely by Monday, so hang in there and remember to stay optimistic."

"You bet I am," said Hope. "It's not easy, but I'm doing it. Thank you for the bracelet. It makes a difference. And by the way, I've also been doing the No Complaining Fast with my kids and, surprisingly, it's really working."

"Of course it is," said Joyce, laughing. "It works with everyone. Also try it at family gatherings. Works wonders at Thanksgiving. Could you believe all the people who complain at Thanksgiving? Just crazy! Works everywhere because everyone complains and 90 percent of it is just mindless babble. Pure babble. Remember, focus on the solution, not the problem, and be the change. Change begins with us."

"I'm on the positive road," said Hope.

"Now, that's my girl," assured Joyce. "I'll call you Monday with good news. I'm praying for good news," Joyce cheered as she hung up the phone.

Good News. She hadn't had good news in a long while and decided right then and there that she deserved good news. Yes, she indeed deserved some good news and after the most painful and difficult year of her life, she was ready for all sorts of good news. And the good news would start with the presentation today. She picked up her computer and bag and headed to the meeting room with confidence and determination to face some professional complainers.

Chapter 19

The Meeting

The usual suspects were there: Dan, Jim, Ken, Wayne, and Robert, who was back from his meeting overseas. It was good to see Robert and his friendly face. He always shared a smile and a kind word whenever he saw her. He reminded Hope a lot of Dan, and she always believed that if Dan ever decided to take a less active role in the company that Robert would be the perfect person to succeed him as CEO. After all, in spite of all the negativity and morale problems, Robert managed to keep his sales team positive and united. He told his team that they couldn't control the battery problems or the fact that there were operational and organization issues, but they could continue to develop relationships with their customers and continue to serve their needs. He believed in a "do whatever it takes" attitude to serve his customers, and he preached this constantly to his sales and customer service people. Robert knew that athough the product matters, it was always about relationships and people. His job was to get the right people on the bus and keep them positive and energized. And his sales team's job was to continue to develop loyal relationships with their customers and serve them.

Hope smiled at Robert and he smiled back, which was a good thing because as she looked around the room, Jim could barely look at her. He just stood there, shaking his head as she set up her laptop and gathered her notes. Dan began the meeting by thanking Hope for all her hard work in preparing the information she was about to share in such a short and critical time frame. Then he said, "Take it away!" to Hope.

Chapter 20

Positive Principles

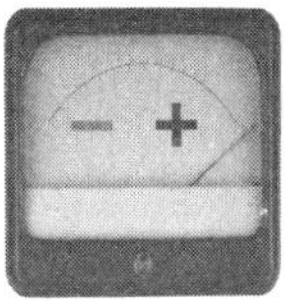

Hope started the meeting with a question. "Why aren't people more positive?" No one seemed to have an answer, and many wondered where Hope was going with this. Hope continued, "I think we would agree that everyone wants to be more positive. And yet so few are. I've been doing a lot of thinking on this and believe that the reason is that it's not a habit. Most of us haven't ingrained positive habits, positive actions, and positive thinking into our lives. So when we face problems, obstacles, and stress we take the negative road instead of the positive road. Well, it's the same with our company. We all talk about being a positive, productive company. We've read all the new books and research demonstrating that positive people, positive interactions, and positive work cultures produce positive results. And yet we have to wonder why are there not more people skipping through our halls, smiling at coworkers, singing "Kumbaya," and loving their jobs? Why do more people die Monday morning at 9 A.M. than at any other time? Why does negativity cost companies $300 billion a year, according to the Gallup Organization? And why do so many companies have morale and productivity challenges?" No one had an answer, but everyone was now paying attention.

"The answer is this: Successful, positive companies with positive employees and positive cultures are created like anything else. Through a set of principles, processes, systems, and habits that are ingrained in the corporate culture and each individual employee. Positive companies aren't born. They are developed. So, let's talk about the key principles." Hope tapped a computer key and pulled up the first slide in her presentation.

A Positive Environment and Culture Are Everything

"It doesn't happen by osmosis," she said. "It happens by relentlessly focusing on our culture and weeding out negativity. As Dan said the other day, negativity is the problem, and we will have to let go of our negative employees who hurt our productivity."

"Like the bloggers," Jim said. "We should have fired both of them, not just one of them," he sneered.

Hope looked right at Jim. "Not really, Jim. You see, the best way to deal with negativity is to create a positive culture where negativity can't breed, grow, and survive. Otherwise, you will spend all your time fighting negativity rather than cultivating a positive culture." Hope brought up the second slide.

Positive Leadership Is Required

"We need positive leadership to build a positive culture. It must be a priority," she said, as she looked at Jim. "Let's face it, we've brought in speakers before who talk about this, but many of us didn't even attend. Our employees got excited, but we didn't ingrain the great ideas they heard into our company DNA. Positive energy flows from the top down in our organization. It trickles up and moves sideways, but it flows from the top down. Positive leadership is essential," she said, raising her voice as Jim rolled his eyes. Hope pulled up the next slide.

The Secret to Winning

"When it comes to building a successful company, there is no debate between nature or nurture. It's all about nurture. We must relentlessly make our culture and people a priority at all levels of our organization. It's like the root and fruit of a tree. The root, which is our culture, people, and spirit must be our focus. Instead of focusing so much on the fruit—profits, stock price, and numbers—let's relentlessly nurture our root. If we do this, we will be very pleased with our fruit."

"But we are a business," countered Jim. "How can you say we shouldn't focus on numbers? We are a public company. We are measured by our numbers."

"Great point," countered Hope. "I'm not saying we shouldn't measure our success. Of course we have to look at numbers. But it shouldn't be our focus. Because people deliver the numbers, people should be our focus, and if we focus on them they will deliver the numbers we want."

Dan was smiling, nodding his head in agreement as he joined the conversation. "You hit the nail on the head, Hope. It's the same philosophy as my mentor John Wooden. As the legendary UCLA basketball coach, he never focused on winning. He focused on developing his players. He focused on improving their fundamentals, skills, character, and teamwork. He focused on people instead of outcomes and as a result he won . . . a lot. Of course the goal of all successful people and teams is to win. But winning is just a goal and not the focus. Winning is the by-product of great effort, leadership, coaching, teamwork, and positive energy. It really is the secret to winning. Please continue," he said, as Jim looked away in disgust.

Trust Must Permeate the Organization

"The number one thing our employees and customers want to know is *Can I trust you, and do you care about me?* Quite frankly our people don't trust us anymore, and we see the effect of that with all these problems we are facing."

"So what should we do? Hold their hands and tell them we love them?" asked Jim as everyone laughed.

"If that's what it takes," answered Hope. "Or simply say what you are going to do and do what you say. If you lead with truth, success will follow. And to spread trust and positive energy throughout the organization we must communicate, communicate, communicate. Which leads me to the next principle."

Fill the Void with Positive Communication

"As Dan mentioned, we must also continue to fill the voids so negativity can't breed," said Hope.

"This is done through positive communication and positive interactions. We can't just allow them to happen by chance. We must ingrain this into our daily process. For example, we should create a daily briefing and post it on our intranet to communicate all aspects of our business to our employees. As leaders, we need to do a better job of listening to our people and empowering them to create solutions. We need to praise them more instead of always demoralizing them. The key is the power of positive interactions. In fact, John Gottman's pioneering research found that marriages are much more likely to succeed when the couple experiences a 5:1 ratio of positive to negative interactions; whereas, when the ratio approaches 1:1, marriages are more likely to end in divorce. Additional research also shows that work groups with positive to negative interaction ratios greater than 3:1 are significantly more productive than teams that do not reach this ratio."

"So you're saying I should never call out an employee when he or she isn't performing. That's ridiculous," said Jim.

Wayne also chimed in. "Are you saying I shouldn't call a stupid idea stupid when I hear it?"

"Not at all," said Hope. "Of course we will have negative interactions. There is research by Barbara Fredrickson from the University of Michigan that shows if a work group in a company experiences a positive to negative interaction ratio of 13:1, the work group will be less effective. This implies that no one is willing to confront the real problems and challenges that are holding them back. Sometimes we need to confront a situation to move past it and, as we know, ignoring problems that stare us in the face doesn't work. Negative interactions are necessary as long as they occur much less frequently than positive interactions. After all, we don't want a 1:1 ratio, which will lead to a high divorce rate with our employees. We know how much turnover costs us. And this leads us to the final principle that I'd like to share with you all."

Become Solution and Innovation Focused

Hope continued, "With a positive culture that fosters positive communication, we can then use our communication network to become solution and innovation focused. We can listen to our employees and encourage them to share their ideas with us. This includes their complaints. If we listen to them and collect their ideas, we will become a company that harnesses the power of its people. We will turn great ideas into successful innovations, and we will turn problems and complaints into solutions."

Chapter 21

Questions

"Wonderful principles," said Wayne, clapping his hands. "But where is the meat? Where's the action plan? What good is a principle if we can't implement it?"

"Actually, what good is a strategy or action plan if it doesn't follow a guiding principle?" countered Hope. "Once you have your principles in place, then you can align your strategies, actions, and processes with your principles. If we follow the principles, we can identify solutions to enhance our culture in all our departments and business divisions, whether it's HR, sales, customer service, manufacturing, and so on. I intend to help each of you do this in your different departments so that we can ingrain positive energy into who we are and everything we do. But for now I want to introduce you to one solution that we can all use in every division, even Ken in manufacturing, and it's called the No Complaining Rule."

Jim and Ken looked at each other with a look that said they weren't sure if she was serious. Wayne spoke with blunt honesty as always. "You had me for awhile, Hope, but you just lost me. Are you serious?"

"I'm dead serious," said Hope.

"Actually, I like it," said Jim. "For once Hope and I agree. I'm sick of our employees whining about everything. Let's put an end to complaining all together."

Dan, on the other hand, chose to sit quietly and take it all in, letting each person speak.

"I'd have to know more before I judge," said Robert.

"It's not exactly what you think it is, gentlemen. I believe it will be a key element to transforming our culture."

"So, what exactly is the rule?" asked Dan.

"Well, that's just it," said Hope. "I haven't thought it all the way through, but I plan to spend today and all weekend preparing for a complete implementation plan that you can share with the board on Monday."

"So, let me get this straight," said Jim. "You have this great idea that is key to our future, and you haven't thought it all the way through. Just great. I can see it now. We'll have employees complaining on their blogs about the No Complaining Rule."

Everyone laughed except Dan and Hope. Hope didn't say a word. She knew she had the gist of the plan. It just wasn't finished yet. She knew that if she shared a part of the plan without explaining it completely, it would be misunderstood and shot down. She was confident that she could deliver a plan on Monday and looked forward to watching Jim eat crow. But Dan had mixed emotions. On the one hand he was a little anxious about what she was planning. On the other hand, he was deeply impressed with the principles she had just shared and trusted she was on to something. He came to her defense.

"I think Hope has something here. I'm looking forward to listening to your plan on how this can be applied to our company," he said, as he shook Hope's hand. "Let's all give Hope a round of applause for a great presentation and great ideas," he said, as several clapped unwillingly. Jim smiled, but it wasn't for the obvious reasons. It was because he couldn't wait until she failed miserably on Monday and was finally where he thought she should be. Anywhere but at EZ Tech.

Chapter 22

More Traffic

Hope drove home in the usual stop-and-go traffic. But this time she wasn't complaining about clueless drivers. This time she was thankful her presentation went well. However, her gratitude soon turned to fear and self-doubt as she thought about an actual plan of implementation of the No Complaining Rule. Everything is always great in theory, she thought. I've seen enough leadership experts and business professors speak to know that theories and ideas don't always equate to successful business practices. What if I can't translate this great No Complaining idea into an actual process that works? What if it's just a great endeavor to try on your own but it's not actionable in a business setting? What if I can't get people to follow through with it? What if it becomes the joke of the company, or worse? The doubts were swirling around in her head. She thought of Jim, and the mere picture of his face made her angry and even more determined to make it work.

When she arrived home, Lauren was outside with her two best friends. They were all dressed up for their homecoming dance. Just great, Hope thought. When they were young she called them the three musketeers, but now she called them the three complainers. As she stepped out of her car, she prepared herself for the onslaught. But the only onslaught she received were smiles, hellos, and hugs. They were cheerful and kind. Hope wondered if they had been drinking, but she didn't smell anything, thank goodness. She later found out that they were infused with the intoxication of kindness and happiness. Turns out that Lauren told her friends about the No Complaining Rule, and they all decided to be more positive. In fact they committed to being the most positive girls in the school. And their goal was to share the No Complaining Rule with their entire school. When Hope heard the news, her fear about being able to translate the rule into a business setting dissipated. She saw how contagious it was with Lauren and her friends. Just as MySpace and Facebook had been adopted by both young adults and business types, she felt it would be the same with the No Complaining Rule. She just had to figure out how to roll it all out to her company so it could spread and work its magic. Jim is toast, she thought. Toast!

Chapter 23

Sunday

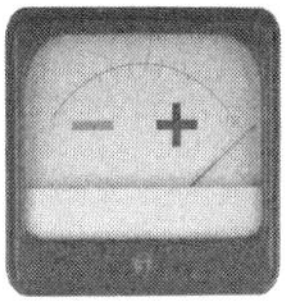

It was Sunday, and Hope found herself sitting in church. As she looked around, she wasn't sure what she was doing there. She stopped going after her husband left a year ago. At the time she felt abandoned, angry, and hurt. This wasn't how her life was supposed to be. She believed that if you were a faithful person, then life would be smooth and happy. But in one moment, her life was rocked to the core. And in that moment she decided that if God was going to allow her life to be destroyed, well then she was going to go it alone. After all, if God wasn't on her side, why should she be on His? Yet here she was sitting in church once again. She didn't know what brought her there. Only that she got up, ate breakfast, got dressed, drove in her car, walked through the doors, and sat down. She didn't even think about it. It was as if she was moved there by some invisible force. And as the music played and Hope mouthed the words to the song she felt a tear come down her face and a familiar feeling in her heart.

The pastor started his talk with a story from the Old Testament. He quoted a passage in the bible where the Israelites were freed from Egypt by Moses. He told how they had spent 400 years as captive slaves, and all at once they were free. At first they were happy and thrilled. But within a month and a half, they started complaining about being hungry. They complained about not having enough water. They complained about living in the wilderness. They even said it would be better to be back in Egypt than slaves free in the desert. Four hundred years of slavery and all it took was a month and a half to start complaining again. Finally, he said, God became so frustrated with all the complaining that He threatened their very existence. Hope smiled and thought: Turns out God is a big fan of the No Complaining Rule. She, of course, knew exactly why she was there today. This message was for her.

The pastor continued, "This story represents the choice we all have. To be positive and free or to be imprisoned by our own negativity. To live in the past or to be hopeful about the future. It's a choice. And only *you* can make it."

Hope thought about her life and knew that she had been given choices many times throughout the year. She saw how she had imprisoned herself from everyone at work and her family at home. But now she was making the right choices again. She knew The No Complaining Rule was a great choice for her. She just hoped it was the right choice for her company.

Chapter 24

Monday

As Hope walked into her office building, she knew she needed to bring the lesson she learned on Sunday in with her. She walked past the security guard on her way to the elevator and gave him a big smile, and he smiled back. She continued walking and then stopped dead in her tracks and walked back to him. "You know, I don't even know your name."

"That's very kind of you," he said. "My name is Walter."

"Well, hello, Walter," Hope said, as she gave him another big smile and continued on to face the executive team.

Dan was getting ready to share his three-point plan via a phone call with the media, and then Hope would present the No Complaining Rule to the executive team. Hope was thrilled when Dan called her over the weekend to let her know that he was going to share Hope's positive principles with the media as part of the three-point plan. He also told her he was looking forward to hearing Hope's plan for the No Complaining Rule and reminded her that he would likely share a general overview with the board at 2 P.M. Hope felt the pressure, but she was ready. Ready to share a powerful way to deal with negativity at work. Ready to make Jim eat crow. Ready to show the executive team that she was back and stronger than ever. Ready to help Dan save EZ Tech. Ready to make her company a more positive place. Ready to prove to herself that she could make an impact. She was so focused on delivering a successful presentation that she didn't even think about her test results. She completely forgot that today was the day when she would hear either good news or bad news about the tests.

Chapter 25

Hope Shares the No Complaining Rule

As Hope stood in front of the executive team, she looked around the room. She couldn't tell if they were smiling because Dan had just delivered a flawless presentation to the media over the phone or because they were amused with her and the topic of complaining. Either way Hope decided that if they wanted to smile, she would give them something to smile about.

Before she began her presentation, she looked at Jim and said, "Now, Jim, as I give my presentation I don't want to hear any complaining. The No Complaining Rule is in effect." Everyone had a good laugh, and Hope continued with an inspirational introduction. She discussed the cost of negativity and why it was essential to build a positive culture. She shared her theory that energy vampires and jerks had to be dealt with in an organization but that a far more dangerous form of negativity was the subtle kind that included complaining, which grew like a cancer. She reiterated the themes she shared on Friday and explained why they were essential to prevent and deal with negativity. Then she shared the No Complaining Rule.

Employees are not allowed to mindlessly complain to their coworkers. If they have a problem or complaint about their job, their company, their customer, or anything else, they are encouraged to bring the issue to their manager or someone who is in a position to address the complaint. However, the employees must share one or two possible solutions to their complaint as well.

Hope reasoned that an employee should never complain to someone who is not able to help with a solution. Mindless complaining serves no purpose and only sabotages morale and performance. Mindless complaining cultivates negativity and adversely affects the complainer and the person being complained to. She further reasoned, to the nodding of everyone in the room, that by encouraging their employees to think of possible solutions to their complaints, employers are empowered to become problem solvers rather than problem sharers. Instead of just riding on the bus, they become a driver of the bus. Instead of causing flat tires, they drive their company on the positive road to success. The result would be a fleet of bus drivers where each person was empowered to create positive change.

She added that *trust* is a significant component of the No Complaining Rule. Leaders and managers must foster the trust of their employees so that employees feel comfortable sharing their complaints and ideas with them. "If we are going to prohibit mindless complaining, then it is essential that we provide an outlet and process of communication for our people to share their complaints, ideas, and solutions. Our employees must know we listen to them, hear them, care about them, and will seriously consider their ideas. If we are going to discourage negative behavior and complaining, then we must do everything possible to encourage positive behavior and positive communication. And that's why the principles I shared on Friday are so important. Without them the No Complaining Rule will not work."

She then added that she believed the No Complaining Rule would be very effective because it is a contagious idea that can be easily ingrained in the culture and habits of each employee and encourages positive solutions instead of negative energy. "As we roll this out, people will learn that in every complaint is a solution waiting to be discovered that will make us better, stronger, and more successful. It will influence every area of our business and generate solutions in logistics, operations, customer service, sales, etc."

"But we don't know for sure if this will work, do we?" asked Jim.

"No, we don't," said Hope, "but I believe it is well worth a shot. Don't you?" she said, as they stared at each other.

"Are you willing to bet your job on this?" Jim asked. Hope thought for a moment as her heart began to pound and her throat became instantly dry. After what seemed like an eternity of silence, she responded, "Yes, I am. I am willing to bet my job. Are you willing to bet your job that it won't work?"

Jim looked around the room as he moved uncomfortably in his chair. "No, I'm not," he said to the amusement of everyone in the room. They were shocked with the way Hope stood up to Jim and were even more shocked that Jim backed down.

Dan particularly didn't care for Jim's approach to people, but he also knew that Jim was important to have on the executive team. He questioned everything and always played the devil's advocate. He never undermined Dan's authority in public but always grilled him on his decisions in private. Dan knew he needed someone like him on his team. He didn't always take his advice, but he knew Jim's style always led to a better decision. He did decide, however, that Jim needed to have less of an influence on the culture and people of his organization. He knew Jim's strengths and developing a positive team was not one of them. He would use Jim to help the organization in different ways.

"So, how do we roll this out?" Jim asked.

Hope smiled at Jim and then at everyone else. "Wouldn't you know it. I happen to have a plan for this as well," she said. "This is the part I wanted to really think through over the weekend and, thankfully, I have some answers." Yes, Hope had answers, but it would take the commitment of everyone on the executive team and in the organization to make the plan work.

Chapter 26

The Rollout

"I've created an Action Plan for each one of us to follow," she said. [The Action Plan can be found in the back of this book.] "Each one of us will meet with the leaders and managers of our departments and divisions. Then we will instruct each manager to meet with his or her team until everyone in the organization has a clear understanding of our approach, rationale, and plan. In addition, everyone in the company will be given a card with the three No Complaining Tools on it," she said, as she handed each member of the executive team a card just like the one Joyce gave her. "Then we will designate a week as No Complaining Week. This will be done to have some fun and help bring awareness to our plan and also make people aware of their own thoughts and mindless complaining. Most importantly, we will relentlessly stress to everyone in the organization that we still want justified complaints to help us develop innovative solutions.

"Each executive and manager will be expected to keep a list of complaints and solutions presented by their employees. They will be instructed to implement obvious solutions within their domain and control. For the suggestions that cannot be resolved immediately or are not within their domain or control, they will be expected to present them either at a managers' meeting or at a quarterly meeting. As you can see, we will become a company that turns complaints into solutions. We will become a company that listens to the ideas, suggestions, and solutions of our people, and we will become a better company as a result. And this concludes my presentation," Hope said, to the enthusiastic applause of her team. They weren't complaining. They were complimenting her for a job well done. Dan had known she was the right person for the job, and now so did everyone else. She was plucked off the bench, put in the game, and she performed brilliantly. Dan knew they would need more solutions in addition to the No Complaining Rule but at least for now he had an overview and framework to share with his board of directors later that day. He also knew that the company had a solid plan to begin the process of turning negative energy into positive solutions and positive change. Thanks to Hope, they were on the road to success, and as a result Dan asked her to join him for the meeting with the board of directors.

Chapter 27

Play to Win

Hope returned to her office, sat in her chair, took a deep breath, and exhaled forcefully. She was both energized and exhausted at the same time. Excited about what she had accomplished but physically drained because of it. She felt the way she used to after a hard fought high school basketball game. Afterward she and her teammates would be so excited about their win but exhausted because they gave everything they had. Her coach always told them to leave everything on the court. "Give it all you've got," he'd say, and that's what she did today. It was the first win she had had in a long time, and she forgot how good it felt.

She didn't play it safe or scared, and she certainly didn't back down to Jim. She played to win. She could hear her coach's words in her head.

> Playing to win requires a commitment to yourself that even if you fail, you will never give up and never let your goals and

dreams die. Those who play to win know that success is not given to us. It is pursued with all the energy and sweat we can muster. Obstacles and struggles are part of life and only serve to make us appreciate our success. If everything came easy, we wouldn't know what it felt like to truly succeed. Obstacles are meant to be overcome. Fear is meant to be conquered. Success is meant to be achieved. They are all part of the game of life and the people who succeed are the ones who play to win, trust, and never give up until the game is over.

Hope smiled and thought of Jim and knew that she definitely played to win today. She knew she had won, but there were many more games yet to be played. The ultimate game—the game of life—was far from over.

Chapter 28

Hope Receives the News

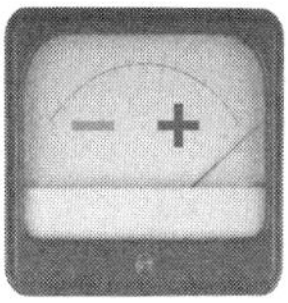

The phone rang, and Hope knew exactly who it was. In all the excitement and preparation for the meeting, she had forgotten all about Joyce and the test results, and yet as soon as the phone rang she instantly knew who it was. She knew by the sound of the ring. She knew because her heart started pounding. She knew because she knew. She shut her office door and answered the phone.

"Hi Joyce," Hope said, nervously.

"Hi, Hope, how are you?" Joyce asked as Hope tried to detect whether the news was good or bad by the tone of Joyce's voice. But she couldn't tell, and after a few seconds of awkward silence Joyce continued.

"So, we have the results."

"Just tell me. I can handle it," Hope cried as her heart began to race faster and she began to shake and perspire.

"You got it," said Joyce as she raised her voice and cheered. "The news is all *good*! Everything is good. The blood work came back good. The ultrasound came back good. It was so good they even had two doctors look at it just to make sure because they didn't want to be wrong. So you are good to go."

It was not what Hope expected to hear, and tears just started to flow down her face. She had tried to be so strong, and now she was allowed to fall apart. She began to cry. And cry and cry. "Thank you. Thank you. Thank you," she said over the phone, but Joyce knew she wasn't thanking her.

"Well, I'm just so happy for you," said Joyce. "I want you to know I'll be thinking about you and, hopefully, we'll see each other again under different circumstances. I know you need to be alone right now. Bye, sweetie."

"Good-bye, and thank you so much," said Hope, as she hung up the phone and collapsed in her chair.

After a few minutes she could feel a certain lightness come over her body. As if she had lost a hundred pounds of fear, stress, and emotional burden. She got up, walked to her office window, and looked out to a beautiful blue sky with a bright full sun. And at that moment a flock of birds flew by. Hope laughed, knowing that this was her personal sign that miracles happen every day. She walked back to her computer and clicked on her music icon. She clicked to her favorite song, raised the volume as loud as possible, and danced around her office.

Chapter 29

Six Months Later

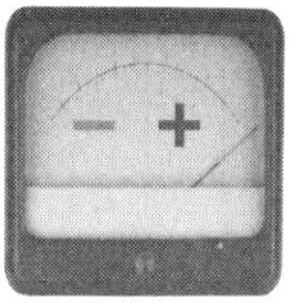

The one thing everyone noticed about the No Complaining Rule was the positive ripples it created. The direct effect was that people were more positive and solution focused. But the ripple effect was probably even more powerful. Everyone agreed that the rule generated the kind of positive energy and culture that attracts higher caliber employees who want to work in a positive environment. It also helped weed out negative employees since they just didn't fit in anymore. The company also spent less time kicking people off the bus, since most of the "wrong" people just got off by themselves. Even better was the fact that most of the wrong people stayed off the bus in the first place. Because managers talked about the No Complaining Rule during the hiring process, it scared most of the "wrong" people away. Over time the company knew this process would create a perpetual cycle of positive energy that would lead to sustained and long-term success. Sure, they couldn't measure the benefit of this positive ripple, but they could measure their growth and the number of satisfied employees via engagement surveys. A recent survey indicated that the percentage of people who said they trusted the executives and managers of the company rose by more than 30 percentage points over the previous year. And the number of people who said they were energized by their work also grew substantially.

But Hope didn't need numbers to prove anything. She saw it firsthand in the employees she worked with every day. Many of them had stopped being passengers on the bus and had become drivers instead.

The web development team told her they created a web site, www.NoComplainingRule.com, to share resources and tools with others.

The marketing team presented to her an "Are You a Complainer?" assessment with five questions that identified whether someone was a complainer or not. They posted the complainer assessment online at www.NoComplainingRule.com and 70 percent of their employees completed the assessment. (The Are You a Complainer? Assessment can be found at the end of this book on page 133.)

A group of engineers worked nights to create a system that automated the complaining and solution process. Now employees could post their complaints and solution ideas, and everyone would know when a complaint was resolved and a solution was implemented.

And her favorite solution of all was brought to her by three twentysomethings from the leadership development program. They said that if we as a company are going to do a No Complaining week, then we have to give people some ideas of what they could do instead of complain. They felt the three No Complaining Tools were helpful, but they suggested that people could benefit from specific practices that empowered people to focus on the positive rather than the negative. The best way to stop a bad habit, they said, is to replace it with a good habit. So they created a card with five things to do instead of complain. The card looked like this (please turn the page):

Five Things to Do Instead of Complain

1. **Practice Gratitude.** Research shows that when we count three blessings a day, we get a measurable boost in happiness that uplifts and energizes us. It's also physiologically impossible to be stressed and thankful at the same time. Two thoughts cannot occupy our mind at the same time. If you are focusing on gratitude, you can't be negative. You can also energize and engage your coworkers by letting them know you are grateful for them and their work.
2. **Praise Others.** Instead of complaining about what others are doing wrong, start focusing on what they are doing right. Praise them and watch as they create more success as a result. Of course, point out their mistakes so they can learn and grow, but make sure you give three times as much praise as criticism.
3. **Focus on Success.** Start a success journal. Each night before you go to bed, write down the one great thing about your day. The one great conversation, accomplishment, or win that you are most proud of. Focus on your success, and you'll look forward to creating more success tomorrow.
4. **Let Go.** Focus on the things that you have the power to change, and let go of the things that are beyond your control. You'll be amazed that when you stop trying to control everything, it all somehow works out.
5. **Pray and Meditate.** Scientific research shows that these daily practices reduce stress; boost positive energy; and promote health, vitality, and longevity. When you are faced with the urge to complain or you are feeling stressed to the max, stop, be still, plug-in to the ultimate power, and recharge.

Chapter 30

It's All Good

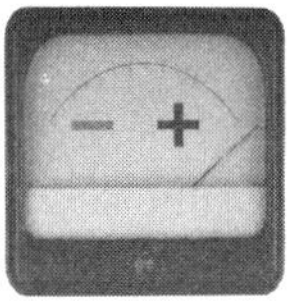

Hope walked out of her building feeling good. She walked past Walter, the security guard, gave him a big smile, and asked how he was doing.

"All good!" he cheered. "It's always good!"

"Wonderful!" she said, as she thought of Joyce and the phone call she received a month ago about her test results. She could still hear Joyce's words in her head, "The news is all good. Everything is good. The blood work came back good."

She shook her head as she thought about the most difficult year of her life. If someone had told her 10 months ago that right now she would be one of the most respected people at EZ Tech; that her teenagers would be thriving, especially Lauren; that she would be training for a marathon; and that her future was brighter than ever, she would have laughed out loud. And yet here she was, enjoying work and life more than ever. She and EZ Tech were back and at the top of their game.

As Hope walked toward her car, she thought of all the bad she had experienced, and it occurred to her that both good experiences and bad experiences lead to good. She noticed it all the time with friends, family, and in the biographies of her greatest heroes, and now she saw it in her own life. She realized that out of tragedy and heartbreak, she found her spirit. Out of struggle she found the courage and faith to move on. And in the face of her own challenges, she found the strength and compassion to make a difference and help save her company. Her husband leaving her surely rocked her world, but it gave her the opportunity to discover the most authentic, most powerful version of herself and become the woman she was born to be. Yes, out of bad emerges good.

And as Hope drove down the street, she remembered reading an article that presented research to support this. The article said that the Gallup Organization conducted a poll asking people what was the worst thing that ever happened to them. Then the pollsters asked the same people what was the best thing that ever happened to them. The pollsters found an 80 percent correlation between the worst and best experiences. The article also pointed out a British study of 400 people who supposedly lived charmed lives. To the outside world, these people had it all and nothing bad ever happened to them. What researchers found was that it wasn't that bad things didn't happen to them, but rather when bad fortune struck they turned it into good. Eventually, it all became good.

She knew that she could never stop bad things from happening but decided that from now on she would turn her complaints into solutions and her misfortune into fortune. She would teach her employees and family to do the same. She pulled a notepad out of the glove compartment as she was waiting at a red light to make the left turn into the hospital and wrote down some notes to share with her daughter, Lauren. She wrote:

1. Trust in a bigger plan.

2. Find strength in adversity.

3. Failure today leads to success tomorrow.

4. The worst event in life is often a catalyst for the best.

5. Positive or Negative. The choice is ours.

When the light turned green, Hope turned into the hospital entrance. She parked her car in her usual spot and walked cheerfully into the building. She walked past the patient area, smiling and greeting both the staff and patients. She made her way to Joyce's office and stopped to say hello as she had every Monday afternoon for the past three months. Joyce showed Hope the stack of *Five Things to Do Instead of Complain* cards and told her they were handing them out. They hugged, and Hope continued on to the hospice section of the hospital where she would spend an hour reading to various patients. She didn't *have* to do it. She felt it was something she *got* to do. She felt she was given a second chance and wanted to help those who weren't as fortunate. She had always hated hospitals but now coming here once a week after work gave her an entirely new perspective. Besides, by volunteering her time she gave the hospice nurses, who Hope considered angels on earth, a well-deserved break.

On her way home, Hope thought about her children. She thought about how resilient they were. She realized how much her attitude and teaching influenced them. And for a moment she thought about her own mortality, which everyone does at certain times in their life. She decided that the greatest gift she could give them would not be wealth or material things but rather the gifts she could leave in them. In their hearts, in their minds, in their attitudes toward life. It would be the same way at work. She couldn't control who stayed and who left EZ Tech. But what she could control was how she affected each person who spent time working there. She could leave an imprint on them and hopefully whatever they did and wherever they went, they would take her positive strategies with them. She would never be a world leader, ambassador, or CEO, but she knew that if she could empower people to turn their complaints and problems into solutions, then in some small way she would be doing her part to change her employees, her company, and, ultimately, the world.

Hope arrived home, walked in the door, and to her great surprise was greeted by Lauren and Jack. They walked her to the kitchen where dinner waited on the stove. A tear ran down her cheek as she read the note sitting on her plate. *For the best mom in the world. We love you.*

Hope hugged and squeezed them as hard as she could. She sat down, and for the first time since Mother's Day five years ago, her kids served her a meal. They told her to enjoy, and when the meal was over, to go relax and watch television because *they* were doing the dishes. Then they all sat down around the table and ate as they discussed the positive things that happened to them at work and school. And as her children shared their stories, Hope looked at them the way only a mother could look at her children and ate the meal they prepared. The food, not surprisingly, wasn't very good. But to Hope it didn't matter at all. It was the moment, not the food, she wanted to savor. And besides, she wasn't about to complain.

Chapter 31

No Complaining Rule Action Plan

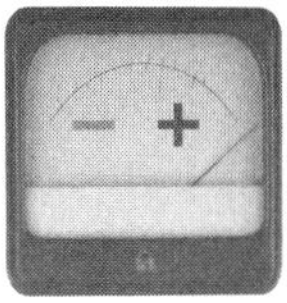

Use this plan to introduce, explain, and implement the No Complaining Rule and empower your team to turn problems into positive solutions. It's a practical and powerful approach for businesses, organizations, schools, churches, sports teams, and even families.

Step 1: Explain the Cost of Negativity and Complaining

Gather your team or organization in person or on the phone and explain the cost of personal and organizational negativity. Use the research and statistics (found on pages 28 and 29) and clearly identify the problem and the effect it has on productivity, performance, and success.

Step 2: Share and Explain the No Complaining Rule

People are not allowed to mindlessly complain to their coworkers and/or team members. If they have a problem or complaint about their job, their organization, their customers, or anything else, they are encouraged to bring the issue to their manager or someone who is in a position to address the complaint. However, the employee or team member must also have thought of one or two possible solutions to the complaint and share that as well.

Exercise

- Discuss the rationale behind the No Complaining Rule.
- Ask people to identify and explain the benefits this rule would likely generate.

Step 3: Justified Complaining versus Mindless Complaining

Discuss the difference between mindless complaining and justified complaining (explained on page 49, the third No Complaining Tool). Explain that mindless complaining focuses on problems whereas justified complaining focuses on solutions.

Exercise

- Discuss the benefits to an organization or team that is solution focused instead of problem focused.
- Have each person draw a line down the middle of a piece of paper. On the left side have them write down examples of justified complaints and on the right side have them write down mindless complaints.
- Discuss the differences between the two types of complaints.

Step 4: Identify and Share Your Complaint/Solution Process

It is essential that each person in your organization understands how your organization and team will consider and address complaints and turn problems into solutions. There are many possible options, and you simply must decide what works best for your type of organization. Following are some ideas to consider. You may use one or a combination of all of these ideas, depending on the size of your organization, the culture, the type of organization, and other factors.

- **Direct Report.** Many organizations will have their people bring their complaints and solutions to their manager or boss, and they work together to solve the problem.
- **Complaint Czar.** Smaller organizations or divisions may elect to have one person handle complaints and solutions and work with managers and/or team members to implement their ideas.
- **Executive Team.** Complaints that center around organizational issues will be brought to the executive team where problems will be considered and solutions will be implemented quarterly.
- **Complaint Terminator.** Organizations may use technology and an intranet site where employees can post their complaints and solutions.
- **The Good Ole Shoe Box.** Smaller organizations or divisions may elect to have their people write their complaints and solutions on a piece of paper and collect them in a "solution box" "idea box," or "innovation box."

Step 5: Listen, Hear, and Act

For the No Complaining process to work effectively, your people need to know that their complaints and solutions will be heard and considered. Their solutions don't necessarily have to be acted upon, but they will want to know that their ideas were considered. It is essential then that your organization address complaints, consider solutions, and act accordingly. As discussed on pages 75–81, the Positive Principles are necessary for the No Complaining Rule to work.

Step 6: Celebrate Successes

To reinforce the No Complaining Rule and generate a solution-focused culture in your organization, you'll want to celebrate and spotlight the successes of people who turned their complaints into solutions and innovations that benefited the organization. Recognize them and share their success stories with the entire organization. Shine a light on people and the process, and this will encourage more success stories. Don't wait for an annual meeting to do this. Do this continuously throughout the year via e-mail, web site postings, conference calls, and meetings.

Step 7: Monitor and Enforce the No Complaining Rule

Encourage leaders, managers, and everyone in your organization to enforce the No Complaining Rule. Make creating a positive culture everyone's priority. Encourage everyone to weed out negativity when they see it and hear it. Make mindless complaining a cultural taboo in your organization. Ingrain positive energy into the culture and habits of your people.

Step 8: Distribute No Complaining Tools

Ingrain the No Complaining Rule into your culture and help break the habit of complaining by sharing No Complaining Tools with everyone. Here are a few ideas.

- Distribute cards with the No Complaining Rule printed on them.
- Distribute cards with the three No Complaining Tools (page 49) on one side and the Five Things to Do Instead of Complain (page 114) on the other side.
- Post NO COMPLAINING, SOLUTIONS WANTED, and STAY POSITIVE posters in your office, home,

or locker room, for example. Posters can be found at www.NoComplainingRule.com.

- Have each person on your team read this book.

Step 9: Designate a No Complaining Week

After you introduce the No Complaining Rule to your organization or team, you'll want to shine a spotlight on the rule by designating a "No Complaining Week." This is a fun but very powerful way to ingrain the rule into the habits of each person and the culture of the organization. To implement a No Complaining Week, try the following:

- Introduce the No Complaining Rule.
- Make sure everyone has the No Complaining Tools mentioned in Step 8.
- Encourage people to monitor their own thoughts for the week and pay attention to how negative they can be.
- Create a fun reward/punishment process when people do complain. For example, in some organizations people put a dollar into a jar every time they complain. At the end

of the week, they donate the collection to a charity.

- Provide each person with the "No Complaining Week" Personal Action Plan found on the next page.

No Complaining Week Personal Action Plan

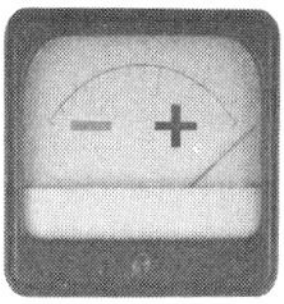

The goal of a No Complaining Week is to become aware of how negative our thoughts and words can be. The objective is to eliminate mindless complaining and negative thoughts as much as possible by replacing them with positive thoughts and positive habits.

Day 1: Monitor Your Thoughts and Words

Spend today monitoring your thoughts and words. You'll be amazed at the thoughts that pop into your head and come out of your mouth. The key is to become more conscious of what you think and say.

Day 2: Make a Gratitude List

When you wake up in the morning, write a list of the things you are thankful for. When you find yourself wanting to complain, focus on what you are grateful for instead.

Day 3: Take a Thank-You Walk

When you wake up in the morning, take a thank-you walk. While you're walking, think of all the things you are grateful for. Try to remember this state of gratitude and carry it with you throughout the day.

Day 4: Focus on the Good Stuff

Today, focus on everything that is right, rather than wrong. Focus on what is right with your life, rather than wrong. Focus on what others are doing right, rather than wrong. Praise instead of criticize. Focus on what you *get* to do versus what you *have* to do.

Day 5: Start a Success Journal

Today, write down all the great interactions and accomplishments you have had today. Do this throughout the day and before you go to bed.

Day 6: Let Go

Make a list of the things you would like to complain about. Go through this list and identify the things that are within your control that you have the power to change and identify those things that are beyond your control. Identify possible solutions and a possible action plan to the things that are within your control. Write the word *surrender* next to the items on your list that are beyond your control.

Day 7: Breathe

Spend 10 minutes in silence. Focus on your breathing while praying or meditating and transform stress into positive energy. Throughout the day, anytime you find yourself feeling stressed or wanting to complain, stop for 10 seconds and breathe. Count your breaths and your blessings.

Are You a Complainer? Assessment

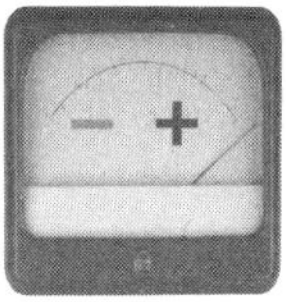

Below are five statements that you may agree or disagree with. Read each one and then select the response that best describes how strongly you agree or disagree.

1. I usually share my problems with others.

7. Strongly Agree
6. Agree
5. Slightly Agree
4. Neither Agree nor Disagree
3. Slightly Disagree
2. Disagree
1. Strongly Disagree

2. I regularly express my negative feelings to others.

7. Strongly Agree
6. Agree

5. Slightly Agree
4. Neither Agree nor Disagree
3. Slightly Disagree
2. Disagree
1. Strongly Disagree

3. I focus more on the causes of problems than on their solutions.

7. Strongly Agree
6. Agree
5. Slightly Agree
4. Neither Agree nor Disagree
3. Slightly Disagree
2. Disagree
1. Strongly Disagree

4. If my life was made into a movie, I would characterize it as a drama instead of a love story, comedy, or inspirational tale.

7. Strongly Agree
6. Agree
5. Slightly Agree
4. Neither Agree nor Disagree
3. Slightly Disagree

2. Disagree
1. Strongly Disagree

5. I complain a lot.

7. Strongly Agree
6. Agree
5. Slightly Agree
4. Neither Agree nor Disagree
3. Slightly Disagree
2. Disagree
1. Strongly Disagree

Now, tally your score by adding the numbers that correspond to each answer. For example, if you answered "Strongly Agree" for all five questions your total would be $7 + 7 + 7 + 7 + 7 = 35$.

35–30: You are a major complainer. Complaining has become a habit for you and it's time to do a No Complaining Fast and action plan.

29–24: You are a complainer. You spend too much time on the Complain Train. Get on the Energy Bus instead.

23–18: You're in the middle of the road. Shift gears, focus on the positive, and spend more time on the positive road.

17–12: Complaining isn't much of an issue for you. Stay Positive.

11–6: You almost never complain. Keep cultivating and sharing the positive energy.

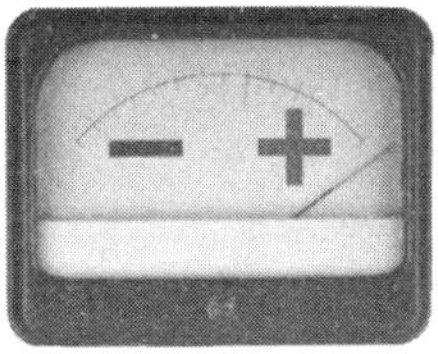

Negative or Positive

Which will you choose?

The No Complaining Rule:
Positive Ways to Deal with Negativity at Work
www.NoComplainingRule.com

Visit www.NoComplainingRule.com to:

- Print a page featuring the No Complaining Rule.
- Print No Complaining posters.
- Invite a coworker or friend to take part in a No Complaining Week.
- Print pages featuring the Three No Complaining Tools and Five Things to Do Instead of Complain.

Visit **www.TheEnergyBus.com** to:

- Send bus tickets via e-mail to your company, organization, school, team, family, and friends and invite them to share the energy
- Print customized bus tickets to mail or hand deliver
- Launch, announce, and garner support for a new initiative
- Enhance individual and group morale, productivity, and performance

If you are interested in leadership, sales, customer service and team-building programs based on *The Energy Bus* principles, **contact The Jon Gordon Companies** at:

830-13 A1A N.
Suite 111
Ponte Vedra Beach, FL 32082
info@jongordon.com
(904) 285-6842

Sign up for Jon Gordon's weekly e-newsletter at **www.jongordon.com.**

Follow him on Twitter at @JonGordon11.

Other Books by Jon Gordon

The Energy Bus
A man whose life and career are in shambles learns from a unique bus driver and set of passengers how to overcome adversity. Enjoy an enlightening ride of positive energy that is improving the way leaders lead, employees work, and teams function.

www.TheEnergyBus.com

Training Camp
This inspirational story about a small guy with a big heart, and a special coach who guides him on a quest for excellence, reveals the eleven winning habits that separate the best individuals and teams from the rest.

www.TrainingCamp11.com

The Shark and the Goldfish
Delightfully illustrated, this quick read is packed with tips and strategies on how to respond to challenges beyond your control in order to thrive during waves of change.

www.SharkandGoldfish.com

Soup
The newly appointed CEO of a popular soup company is brought in to reinvigorate the brand and bring success back to a company that has fallen on hard times. Through her journey, discover the key ingredients to unite, engage, and inspire teams to create a culture of greatness.

www.Soup11.com

The Seed
Go on a quest for the meaning and passion behind work with Josh, an up-and-comer at his company who is disenchanted with his job. Through Josh's cross-country journey, you'll find surprising new sources of wisdom and inspiration in your own business and life.

www.Seed11.com

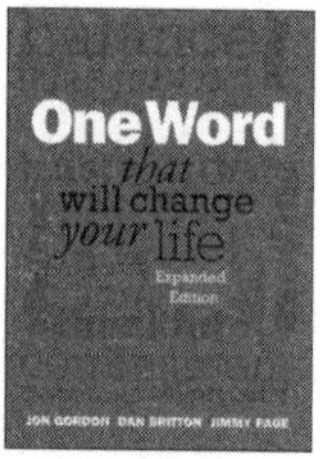

One Word

One Word is a simple concept that delivers powerful life change! This quick read will inspire you to simplify your life and work by focusing on just one word for this year. *One Word* creates clarity, power, passion, and life-change. When you find your word, live it, and share it, your life will become more rewarding and exciting than ever.

www.getoneword.com

The Positive Dog

We all have two dogs inside of us. One dog is positive, happy, optimistic, and hopeful. The other dog is negative, mad, pessimistic, and fearful. These two dogs often fight inside us, but guess who wins? The one you feed the most. *The Positive Dog* is an inspiring story that not only reveals the strategies and benefits of being positive, but also an essential truth: being positive doesn't just make you better; it makes everyone around you better.

www.feedthepositivedog.com

The Carpenter

The Carpenter is Jon Gordon's most inspiring book yet—filled with powerful lessons and success strategies. Michael wakes up in the hospital with a bandage on his head and fear in his heart after collapsing during a morning jog. When Michael finds out the man who saved his life is a carpenter, he visits him and quickly learns that he is more than just a carpenter; he is also a builder of lives, careers, people, and teams. In this journey, you will learn timeless principles to help you stand out, excel, and make an impact on people and the world.

www.carpenter11.com

The Hard Hat

A true story about Cornell lacrosse player George Boiardi, *The Hard Hat* is an unforgettable book about a selfless, loyal, joyful, hard-working, competitive, and compassionate leader and teammate, the impact he had on his team and program, and the lessons we can learn from him. This inspirational story will teach you how to build a great team and be the best teammate you can be.

www.hardhat21.com

You Win in the Locker Room First

Based on the extraordinary experiences of NFL Coach Mike Smith and leadership expert Jon Gordon, *You Win in the Locker Room First* offers a rare, behind-the-scenes look at one of the most pressure-packed leadership jobs on the planet, and what leaders can learn from these experiences in order to build their own winning teams.

www.wininthelockerroom.com

Life Word

Life Word reveals a simple, powerful tool to help you identify the word that will inspire you to live your best life while leaving your greatest legacy. In the process, you'll discover your *why*, which will help show you how to live with a renewed sense of power, purpose, and passion.

www.getoneword.com/lifeword

The Power of Positive Leadership

The Power of Positive Leadership is your personal coach for becoming the leader your people deserve. Jon Gordon gathers insights from his bestselling fables to bring you the definitive guide to positive leadership. Difficult times call for leaders who are up for the challenge. Results are the byproduct of your culture, teamwork, vision, talent, innovation, execution, and commitment. This book shows you how to bring it all together to become a powerfully positive leader.

www.powerofpositiveleadership.com

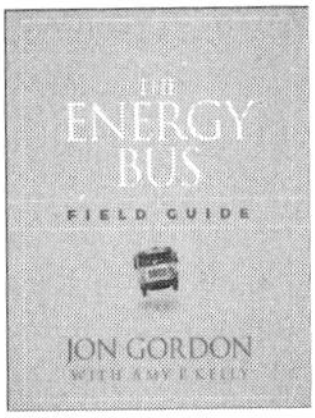

The Energy Bus Field Guide

The Energy Bus Field Guide is your roadmap to fueling your life, work, and team with positive energy. The international bestseller, *The Energy Bus*, has helped millions of people from around the world shift to a more positive outlook. This guide is a practical companion to help you *live and share* the ten principles from *The Energy Bus* every day, with real, actionable steps you can immediately put into practice in your life, work, team, and organization.

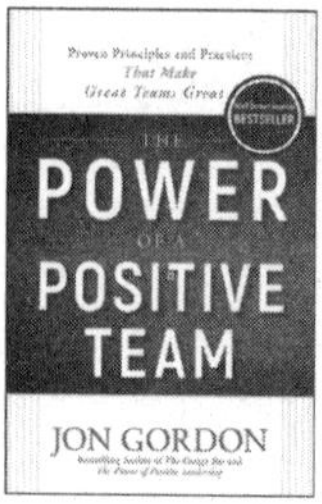

The Power of a Positive Team
In *The Power of a Positive Team*, Jon Gordon draws upon his unique team building experience, as well as conversations with some of the greatest teams in history, to provide an essential framework of proven practices to empower teams to work together more effectively and achieve superior results.

www.PowerOfAPositiveTeam.com

The Coffee Bean
From bestselling author Jon Gordon and rising star Damon West comes *The Coffee Bean:* an illustrated fable that teaches readers how to transform their environment, overcome challenges, and create positive change.

The Energy Bus for Kids
The illustrated children's adaptation of the bestselling book, *The Energy Bus*, tells the story of George, who, with the help of his school bus driver, Joy, learns that if he believes in himself, he'll find the strength to overcome any challenge. His journey teaches kids how to overcome negativity, bullies, and everyday challenges to be their best.

www.EnergyBusKids.com

Thank You and Good Night
Thank You and Good Night is a beautifully illustrated book that shares the heart of gratitude. Jon Gordon takes a little boy and girl on a fun-filled journey from one perfect moonlit night to the next. During their adventurous days and nights, the children explore the people, places, and things they are thankful for.

The Hard Hat for Kids
The Hard Hat for Kids is an illustrated guide to teamwork. Adapted from the bestseller *The Hard Hat*, this uplifting story presents practical insights and life-changing lessons that are immediately applicable to everyday situations, giving kids—and adults—a new outlook on cooperation, friendship, and the selfless nature of true teamwork.

www.HardHatforKids.com

Index